TALE *of*
TWO TERMS

GOVERNING IN GOOD TIMES AND BAD

By GOVERNOR CHRIS GREGOIRE

with Fred Olson

Print Edition ISBN: 978-1-889320-32-8
EPUB Edition ISBN: 978-1-889320-33-5
MOBI Edition ISBN: 978-1-889320-34-2

Front cover photo by Weldon Wilson
Spine photo by Kari Blunck, Studio K
Back cover portrait by Michele Rushworth
Dedication page photo by La Vie Photography, Seattle WA

Printed in the United States of America
By Gorham Printing, Centralia, WA

Not printed at government expense

To my husband, Mike,

my daughter Courtney, her husband Scott Lindsay,

my wonderful new granddaughter Audrey Christine Lindsay,

and my daughter Michelle,

whose love and support made it

possible for me to pursue my passion

for public service.

CONTENTS

INTRODUCTION

I WAS READING THROUGH MY MAIL a number of years ago when I came across a letter from a woman in a small Eastern Washington town.

"You probably don't remember me," she wrote. She went on to explain that as a young lawyer for Washington's Office of the Attorney General, I had helped her and her husband adopt a young girl who was in their foster care.

The woman told me her family had followed my career and were excited when I became attorney general. Her daughter had grown up and recently graduated from Eastern Washington University with a degree in social work. She was writing, she said, to tell me that, because of my influence all those years ago, her daughter had decided to get her law degree and help children much like I had done.

I have always remembered that letter. Sure, it was gratifying to see I had a small role in helping shape the life of a young girl. But more importantly, it reminds me that helping others make a better life for themselves is why I chose a career in public service.

My own adolescence was shaped by my mom, a single parent who worked as a short-order cook. It wasn't easy for her, balancing a hard job with raising a daughter. I remember going to the restaurant on Saturdays and sitting on a stool in the kitchen doing my homework and watching mom work. I learned a lot about what working hard means from her.

I still remember when one restaurant was going through hard times and the owner couldn't pay her. He urged her to keep working and promised he would pay her in a few weeks when business picked up. In a few weeks, however, she showed up for work and found a padlock on the door. She was out two weeks' pay and unemployed.

Mom taught me about resiliency, the power of love and to set high expectations for myself. Looking back, I realize we didn't have much, but there was always love in the house and mom's most fervent dream—that I would go to college.

Like a lot of kids my age, my passion for public service was shaped by President John F. Kennedy. He inspired so many of us, and his famous inaugural remark, "Ask not what your country can do for you—ask what you can do for your country," still resonates with me.

I have a replica of his famous rocking chair in my office. I understand it helped ease his back pain, and it was so important to him that he always took it with him on Air Force One when he traveled around the world. My replica is my reminder of JFK and is never used, although a few staff members have tried to sit on it and then later joked with me about the glare they received.

When I left for the University of Washington (UW), it is, therefore, no wonder my career focus was on public service. I did dabble for a while with the idea of being a pharmacist, but it didn't take too long to realize I would be terrible at that job. So I turned my attention to education and earned a teaching certificate in the late 1960s—just as schools stopped hiring new teachers.

But life does indeed take interesting turns. The lack of a teaching position sent me scrambling for a job. When I proudly announced to mom that I had found one, she wasn't overly excited to hear I was a clerk typist in one of the toughest probation and parole offices in the state. In fact, it was in an area so unsafe that I was escorted to my car at night.

I still remember one of the first parolees I worked with. He was back in the community after serving time for murder and had been in prison so long that he was struggling to adjust to life on the outside. So I helped him buy clothes, learn to dance, figure out what bus to take and how to deal with many of the other things we all take for granted in our daily lives. Despite his criminal record, he was a kind, gentle man. He completely turned his life around and went on to have a successful career in law enforcement.

Little did I know that I would rise from that entry-level job and become governor. I didn't even think of running for office until about 20 years later when I successfully campaigned for attorney general. I had been too busy in the interim getting a law degree, marrying my husband, Mike, balancing two jobs, raising our daughters, Courtney and Michelle, and then practicing law in the Attorney General's Office.

Along the way I had become even more passionate about public service. First and foremost, I loved doing things that made life better for others. I loved the clash of ideas and philosophies you have to deal with in the public sector, and the challenge of trying to find common ground to create new policies or programs. I loved managing in an environment where everything you do is transparent and you are immediately held accountable for your decisions.

I learned that while the work and decision-making of state government aren't always pretty or efficient, governing is an amazing process that involves considering all the differing views of people in our state.

Not that the people always agree with you. You will never make some people happy. While running for attorney general, I remember meeting an elderly man who grumbled, "No women, no women generals!" Fortunately, those moments are offset by times like the one when I was leaving an elementary school and felt a tug on my sleeve. I looked down at a little boy gazing up at me. "Lady, I want to be just like you when I grow up," he said.

When Governor Gary Locke announced in July 2003 that he wouldn't seek re-election, I was eager to run for his vacant seat. As attorney general, I certainly had a chance to influence public policy, but it was more the case that I was managing a very large public law firm and defending the policies of others. The Governor's Office was a far bigger test of public-sector management.

As it turned out, I barely won the election. In fact, my 133-vote win, after two recounts and a court challenge, was the narrowest, most contentious governor's race in the nation's history. The rancor spilled over into the early days of my four-year term. Some Republicans in the House refused to acknowledge me when I gave my inaugural address. Protestors outside the Capitol chanted "Revote, revote." And there were bumper stickers that read, "She's not my governor."

I didn't enter office in a position of strength, which would have been helpful since I immediately had to deal with a $2.2 billion budget shortfall. Fortunately, the economy pivoted and hummed along for the next three years. By the end of my first year, 85,000 new jobs had been added to the economy, and unemployment was about 5.5 percent by the end of my first term.

With help from the Legislature, we were able to provide health care for tens of thousands more children. We reduced class sizes in our schools. We launched a massive highway construction program, which provided jobs, increased traffic safety and boosted freight mobility—all vital to economic development. We created a new government accountability program and the voters approved a rainy-day fund, which finally forced the state to save for hard financial times. We restructured health care to cut costs and deliver better access and higher-quality care, and we created early learning pro-grams to help more kids succeed in school. We opened branch campuses of the universities and expanded community college enrollment.

Four years later, however, after I had been re-elected by a 194,000-vote margin, my job changed dramatically.

Like other states, Washington was buffeted by the largest economic crisis since the Great Depression. State revenues plummeted by nearly 7 percent. As revenue collections spiraled downward, we made deep cuts to state spending. Year after year—sometimes twice in a year—we had to make agonizing decisions that affected the lives and livelihoods of people across the state. Our job was made even harder as state revenue declined in the downturn—demand increased for such services as health care, food, unemployment and public education.

As the recession deepened and it became clear a recovery wasn't coming anytime soon, I searched for records and accounts from other governors about how they managed through their own stubborn recessions. Other than a few ideas gleaned from inaugural addresses, I was unable to find anything germane to what we were going through in our state. That's where the idea for this collection of reflections was born.

I wanted to capture some of the lessons I learned about governing through the bad times, as well as the good times, too. This isn't intended as a glossy record of the Gregoire years. History will determine how my two terms will be judged. And now, particularly with the Internet, there is ample record of my administration.

This collection is intended as a record for future governors or students of government to see how someone else managed. It is not about the right way or the wrong way to govern; it is simply a record of the challenges I encountered, how I tackled them and the lessons I learned along the way.

I have been humbled by the opportunity to be governor of this great state, and I hope the ideas gathered here help others who share my passion for managing in the public sector.

The French Fry Lady

SOMETIMES a governor has to do things that don't look so gubernatorial.

Consider, for instance, the day in Saigon when I wore an apron and handed out french fries in a KFC.

That night, I made the Saigon television news and was dubbed the "french fry lady" by a reporter.

You wouldn't think a "news" story like that would have much impact, but it did. For the next few days on my trade mission, people pointed at me and, according to my interpreter, they said, "Look, there is the french fry lady."

As a new governor in 2005, I didn't fully understand the vital role that trade missions—even the lighter moments like the french-fry promotion—would play in Washington's economy.

Eight years and 12 trade missions later, I know these international trips are grueling and challenging, but are definitely worth it for Washington businesses and our future.

Trade missions also helped me sharpen my focus on economic development. I like to tell people that I flew into foreign cities on a Boeing airplane. On the drive to the hotel I passed a big Microsoft building. There was a Starbucks across the street from the hotel. And the local Costco looked just like the one in Tumwater, and featured Washington products, such as wine, beef, potatoes and cherries. It's clear that our local businesses and products are known worldwide for their outstanding quality.

Economically, Washington is really more like a small nation than a state.

We export more than twice as much per worker as any other state in the country, and the sky is the limit. Our ports are the gateway to America for goods from Asia. They also serve as a means for exporting our high-quality products, whether they are airplanes, pharmaceuticals, medical products or apples.

We are a state known for quality products, creativity, innovation and an entrepreneurial spirit. Trade, aerospace, technology, life sciences, global health, the military, our research institutions and agricultural products are engines of Washington's economy. I soon learned you need to focus your efforts on your state's strengths and use them to out-compete others.

Trade missions taught me that economic development work requires a governor to play many different roles—saleswoman, barrier buster, mediator, expeditor and problem solver. All those roles are really aimed at doing one thing: providing a foundation (or infrastructure) needed for business to prosper.

The old adage, "Government doesn't create jobs, business creates jobs," is true. But that doesn't mean government isn't a player. Our job is to pave the way for economic development, then move aside. That means making sure business has access to skilled workers. It means having a transportation system that efficiently delivers workers to the job and products to market. In Eastern Washington, it means providing water to turn arid land into a fertile, multi-billion-dollar agricultural region. It means fighting for fair trade to keep foreign markets open and ports accessible. In our mobile and wired world, it means having broadband access in all parts of the state. And it means providing a modern, effective, cost-efficient state government that isn't an anchor on business success, but instead a sail.

Aerospace is, of course, the backbone of Washington's economy, boasting 92,000 jobs and growing. *Forbes* magazine recently listed the Seattle-Bellevue-Everett corridor number one in the nation for growth in manufacturing. Aerospace accounts for half of that expansion.

That is heady but daunting news—daunting because aerospace industries are rapidly changing and will require a growing number of highly skilled workers and engineers. The new Boeing 787, for instance, is a game-changing, carbon-fiber-composite airplane that is 20 percent more fuel efficient.

Washington state's advantage across its primary job sectors is its highly skilled, educated workforce. It is absolutely vital that we remain diligent and competitive in education. To put it another way, higher education is an economic engine for Washington state.

Recognizing the need for new, skilled workers, we joined forces with the private sector and worked with the Legislature to pass education bills to prepare students for jobs of the future. We expanded high school and community college programs aimed at training aerospace workers. We provided funds to produce more engineers at the UW and Washington State University (WSU). And we created research centers at the two universities to develop new technologies for innovative products in aviation, aerospace and defense.

It is one thing to make promises to potentially new Washington businesses; it is another to deliver. One of the questions I was asked most often on trade missions when I was recruiting businesses to come to Washington was whether there would be a skilled workforce available. I told Charlie Earl, the executive director for the State Board for Community and Technical Colleges, that in every case I could confidently say yes. Our community college system is nimble and adaptive and has always come through with the training workers need to be employable.

I remember visiting the Boeing plant in Renton and being stopped by a number of young workers who thanked me for helping them get their jobs. They said my work to help open additional higher-education enrollment slots allowed them to get their degrees and compete for their jobs.

On a visit to the Stade region of Germany, where Airbus has an assembly plant, I toured a building and learned about a partnership called CFK Valley Stade. It is a partnership between regional government, higher education and industry to conduct research and development, as well as train workers on the latest aerospace tools and technology.

It made me think about the Innovation Partnership Zones we have created to encourage similar collaboration around our state. I realized we needed to beef up the statewide research-and-development component for aerospace, so I worked with the Legislature to create startup funding for the

Washington Aerospace Research and Development Center.

With the news that Boeing's 787 would be built in Washington, we set out in 2005 to enhance the supply chain. Our aerospace supplier cluster had about 500 aerospace supply chain companies in 2005, and the number grew to 740 by 2012—the largest, most robust supply chain in the world.

If you had told me about the kind of work being done in the field of life sciences when I graduated from UW in 1969, I doubt that I, or anyone else for that matter, would have realized just how significant an impact life sciences would have on our economy in 2012.

Today, in 70 Washington cities, there are companies, college researchers and nonprofit organizations finding cures for cancer, deciphering the human genome, designing better medical devices and producing more robust crops.

Life sciences have become a huge new business for Washington, adding nearly $10.5 billion to the economy. With 34,000 employees, and average wages more than 60 percent above those typical for the private sector, life sciences companies have continued to grow the past several years.

These new businesses are not only providing lifesaving products here at home, they also are a burgeoning part of our export market. In the past decade, pharmaceutical exports are up 278 percent and medical product exports rose 179 percent. China, Japan, Belgium and Canada are our biggest customers, with exports to China alone reaching $170 million.

We took some innovative steps to nurture this rapidly growing, global-health market in Washington. In 2005, to help provide a foundation for research and development, I convinced the Legislature to set up the Life Sciences Discovery Fund.

To create the fund, we used the bonus money Washington received for my work on the Master Tobacco Settlement Agreement, which I helped negotiate as attorney general. I love the poetry in the idea that we are taking money from companies that produce products that will kill you and instead are using it to assist businesses making products that heal people and reduce suffering.

So far, our $59 million in grants has leveraged nearly $400 million in additional funds from federal, corporate and private sources.

More importantly, there are promising results, including new cancer drugs, faster ways to detect breast cancer recurrence, and improved techniques to help us learn causes and treatments for autism, dyslexia and learning disabilities. In 2010, three of the 21 drugs approved by the federal Food and Drug Administration were discovered and developed in Seattle.

Life Sciences Discovery Fund grants have impacts all across the state.

A (Spokane) *Spokesman-Review* editorial urged the state to continue to fund research in life sciences. As evidence of the value, the paper cited a program at the College of Nursing at WSU-Spokane that is training primary-care doctors in rural counties how to tackle painkiller abuse. "In an urban setting, doctors can turn to mental health professionals to manage such cases. But out in the country, those experts often are not available," the editorial noted.

Washington is home to a robust information and communications technology (ICT) sector. With more than 124,000 employees as of 2011, the ICT sector has recovered all of the jobs lost since 2008, and continues to grow. Companies like Microsoft and Amazon make Washington a hub of innovation, and help Washington compete internationally in the ICT sector.

Past partnerships with the state have resulted in establishing the Opportunity Scholarship Fund, and I actively promote Washington ICT businesses on trade missions.

Obviously, the ICT sector needs highly skilled workers, and I have learned it is critical that we involve industry leaders so we can tailor education programs to meet their needs for today's and tomorrow's jobs.

Trade missions are more than business recruiting opportunities—they also allow us to address issues like intellectual property and privacy, which are vital to the ICT sector.

On one trade mission to China, Nancy Anderson, from Microsoft's Legal and Corporate Affairs group, and I met with the vice-chairman of the Central Government in China—the third-highest ranking official in the country—to talk about intellectual property and privacy. But first he told us (through an interpreter) about taking hikes on Mount Rainier when he was in our state visiting his daughter, who was studying at the University of Washington.

It reminded me how small our world has become.

While on trade missions, I was impressed by the demand for Washington agricultural products. In Korea, I watched as a shipment of Washington cherries was cleared off the shelves in just a few hours.

Today, Washington has 39,000 farms, and the crops and livestock they produce are worth more than $8 billion. Add 2,000 businesses in the food-processing industry and the annual worth jumps another $12 billion.

We are the nation's leading grower of apples, potatoes, milk, beef, cherries, pears, raspberries and mint. Agricultural exports grew in 2011 to more than $8.6 billion and will continue to grow as we add markets like the one in Vietnam for potatoes.

I like to say we are the refrigerator to the world.

Our agricultural-sector strategy was to provide three key things—water, a reliable transportation system and research.

For about 40 years, bitter fighting among farmers, environmentalists, municipalities and others prevented us from more wisely allocating our vital water supply. Finally, in 2006, we negotiated an historic agreement that provided water for farms, fish and families.

The transportation improvements were no less hard fought. With my razor-thin 2004 election victory still being contested in the courts, I supported a gas tax increase to improve our roads. Critics said even if I survived the court challenge, the tax hike would drag me down in the next election. But with the backing of unions and business (they may fight on some issues, but two areas they often agree on are transportation and education), the gas tax squeaked through and then survived an attempt to overturn it at the polls.

The tax provided $16.3 billion to improve our transportation system, including funding for a massive Interstate 90 Snoqualmie Pass project to keep agricultural products moving from Eastern Washington to vital Puget Sound ports.

Eighty years ago, the electrification of our rural areas was critical to improving lives and livelihoods in rural Washington. A few years ago, we completed the equivalent project for the 21st century—bringing high-speed broadband to the entire state.

The high-speed wiring of Washington was done by a private/public partnership, including a coalition of public utility districts. The group developed a comprehensive plan to bring broadband to the state, but was short of funds to complete the work.

Then the recession hit. Yet we found opportunity amid the adversity.

President Obama and Congress offered the states billions of dollars for broadband expansion. And because Washington state had already developed a plan and was ready to go to work, we received $243 million—that equates to 7 percent of the total funds despite only having 2 percent of the nation's population.

With the addition of federal funds to more than $1 billion in private-sector money, we were able to provide 99 percent of our residents with access to high-speed Internet. As a result, Washington has been named the most wired state in the U.S.

The broadband initiative opened doors to economic development at the most basic level. In the small town of Reardan, in Lincoln County, for instance, sisters Pam Soliday and Janet Nesbitt had opened a quilt shop in the carriage house of a local farm. They found, however, the small market couldn't support their business, so they began using the Internet to market their unique quilt supplies and patterns. Today, with social media and electronic newsletters, they are in contact with as many as 15,000 people, including customers from Germany, Italy and Japan.

Just as the recession may have helped us speed up installation of broadband, it was also instrumental in helping us take on another issue essential to economic development—reforming government so it is leaner, more efficient and more cost effective.

As the nation sank deeper and deeper into the recession, I realized we had a critical choice: muddle through as best we could, or reform government and emerge from the recession stronger and more agile. We chose to reform.

We merged agencies to increase efficiency. We eliminated boards and commissions that were no longer needed. We made changes to the public pension plans to make them among the most sustainable in the nation (see chapter on reform).

Two of the biggest costs to business, however, were our workers' compensation and unemployment insurance programs. Both faced skyrocketing costs, which are borne by businesses and workers. Tinkering with the two systems has always been a lightning rod for business and labor interests, so major reform had been quashed for decades. I was convinced, though, that without reform we would have a major drag on our recovery from the recession.

The fight wasn't pretty, but we finally passed reforms that protect workers and contain costs for businesses.

My stint with an apron passing out french fries in Saigon was just one of my sales efforts. I loved promoting Washington's wine industry. My staff would always cringe, but one of my main messages, intended with humor, was, "Washington makes fine wine; California makes jug wine."

I took my wine pitch everywhere, even to the White House, where I convinced First Lady Michelle Obama to serve Washington wines at state dinners.

A governor's job isn't just helping develop new businesses; it is also fighting for today's employers. One of my most satisfying days was Oct. 29, 2012, in Hoquiam, Wa., where I helped celebrate the reopening of Harbor Paper, formerly Grays Harbor Paper Co.

"Today is a celebration of renewal," I told the crowd at the ceremony. "The reopening of Harbor Paper is a positive example of what can happen when the state, private investment and local business come together—they can help rebuild and revive a local economy and community."

The Harbor Paper mill received state funding through Washington's Small Business Credit Initiative, a program announced in December 2011 and operated by the state's Department of Commerce. Small-business own-ers are provided with as much as $5 million in loans to create and preserve jobs in underserved communities. That funding, combined with private investments, helped reopen the mill's doors.

The reopening was a real success for Commerce, which does similar work with communities all around the state.

When I took office, Commerce was called the Department of Community, Trade and Economic Development, or CTED. As staff liked to point out, it was the "junk drawer" of state government without a singular-organizing mandate.

Over the years, legislators liked to put pet programs in the agency be-cause they felt it was a safe harbor for them.

As a result, CTED had programs as diverse as housing assistance, tour-ism, energy assistance, child-care facilities and international trade. Culturally, it was, as staff liked to say, "wing tips vs. Birkenstocks."

As the recession tightened its grip on the state and nation in 2009, CTED Director Julie Wilkerson told me she wanted to retire. I realized it could be the time to move job creation back to the top of the agency's agenda.

I hired Rogers Weed as the new director. Rogers had impressive educa-tion credentials and had spent most of his career at Microsoft.

My direction to Rogers was to focus on job creation and better align state policy and programs with the needs of business. As a first step, I con-vinced the Legislature to both rename the agency Commerce, and direct the agency to study how best to reorganize itself so it could focus on job creation and retention.

Old habits die hard in government. In 2010, we proposed legislation to move 25 programs out of Commerce so it could have a singular focus. But legislators were unable to clean out the "junk drawer," and only agreed to move five programs.

While Commerce is still an agency with many missions, Rogers, with a background in business, has kept jobs as the primary focus and worked to connect the other surviving programs to the agency's mission.

Rogers and Dan Newhouse, my director at the Department of Agriculture, have been my two key trade partners. They soon learned about the pace we would keep while abroad. On June 20, 2011, for instance, our day at the Paris Air Show started at dawn with breakfast and ended at 10 p.m. after 17 meetings or events.

The (Tacoma) *News Tribune* followed local-business owners on our trade mission a year later to the Farnborough Air Show near London. "It was the hardest work I have done in my life," one businessman said. "I'll have to go back someday and see London."

The *News Tribune* story accurately portrayed the pace we set and the business connections we made on trade missions. But not all media coverage was so fair, and it provided an important lesson. Here's what one story said during the 2011 Paris Air Show: "As their cash-strapped governments slashed public programs and shed jobs, records show officials from at least 14 states jetted across the Atlantic in June to attend the Paris Air Show at Le Bourget."

The article went on to report the cost of Washington's trip, including security, was $98,000. The story didn't mention that two Washington firms alone signed contracts worth $2.9 million as a result of meetings conducted during the trade mission.

What's harder to put a measure on is the fact that trade missions break down barriers and open doors for businesses. After all those miles logged on trade missions, I am absolutely convinced trade can't be done with Pacific Rim nations without personal relationships. That means we have to go there and meet people in person. Emails or letters won't work. In Asia especially, it's impossible to get in the door unless you're a leader like a governor.

The first stop I made on our Vietnam trip was to meet governmental leaders, and we found a receptive business climate after that visit.

On various trade missions, Dan and I worked to eliminate tariffs in Korea on french fries and cherries. We convinced Colombian officials to eliminate tariffs on wheat, apples, pears and french fries.

We kept markets open for Washington products ranging from cherries in Japan, fresh potatoes in Mexico and Vietnam, to apples in Taiwan and India, and Kraft linerboard in China.

My work as the "french fry lady" may have been a little offbeat for a governor, but it helped get results. When it comes to chasing down new jobs or business for the state, I know now you have to wear many hats, and, at times, even an apron.

High Expectations

I TRAVELED to a remarkable event in the small Eastern Washington town of Bridgeport, on June 1, 2011, with the U.S. Secretary of Labor, Hilda Solis.

Bridgeport, in the central part of the state and about 70 miles north of Wenatchee, is known for fruit and hydropower. It rests on the Columbia River, adjacent to the giant Chief Joseph Dam and amidst cherry, apple and pear orchards.

Drawn by seasonal work in the orchards, Bridgeport is 75 percent Hispanic. The high school, home of the Mustangs and Fillies, has an enrollment of 200 students, and 91 percent are minorities. Every student in the school is on the free or reduced-price lunch program, which isn't surprising since 98 percent of the student body comes from economically disadvantaged families.

Given the statistics on Bridgeport High, some people would say these students have little chance of success. But they would be very, very wrong.

Bridgeport's graduation rate is more than 82 percent (10 years ago it was 41 percent), and every graduating senior in 2011 was accepted into a college or technical course following graduation. Many of the students are the first in their family to go to high school, let alone college.

Based on the academic achievement of Bridgeport High students, the school was selected as one of six finalists in the nation in 2011 to have President Barack Obama deliver its commencement address.

Bridgeport's principal is Tamra Jackson, who, I am told, also serves as event planner, press contact, security guard and town firefighter.

If you ask Tamra about Bridgeport's success, she'll tell you, "There are no excuses here. You get in, you work hard, and you do your very best."

But even more importantly, Tamra says, "We have high expectations. Students will do well whenever you set high expectations."

In the end, Bridgeport did not win and the President did not attend the graduation. That's where Secretary Solis and I came in. We had the honor of speaking at the graduation for the 37-member Bridgeport Class of 2011.

Attending graduation that day made me think about my mom. She was forced to drop out of high school to help support her family during World War II. She never returned to school and went on to a career as a short-order cook.

I have never understood where it came from, but from my earliest years mom instilled in me an expectation that I would get an education. There was never any question about it. I would work hard in school and go on to college.

Looking back, I think I was as excited for mom as I was for myself when she watched me get my bachelor's degree from UW, and later my Juris Doctor degree from Gonzaga University.

Tamra Jackson at Bridgeport and my mom had it right—we need to set high expectations for our kids. And if we do—accompanied by encouragement, support and attention—they will flourish.

When I arrived in the Governor's Office in January 2005, I found our education system was mired in the 20th century and had not set the high expectations needed for the 21st century.

I realized the education system was not all that different from the one in place when I was a student teacher in the late 1960s.

Back then, most of the jobs were in manufacturing, and the skills you learned carried you through your entire working career. Indeed, many workers joined a company and remained there until they got a retirement watch 40 years later.

Today, you can't be sure your employer will remain in the same business, let alone expect long-term job security. Most jobs are in the service sector, where knowledge is king and science, technology, engineering and math skills are the top career currencies.

I was convinced our education system wasn't preparing our kids for the job markets of today in fields like global health, aerospace, advanced manufacturing and other research-intensive industries. And, while our older workers were relatively well-educated, our younger workers were not. As a result, workers from out of state were coming in to fill some of our best jobs, leaving less-stable, lower-paying jobs for our graduates.

The trends were clear to me. A quality education is not only vital to our children; it is the single most important economic investment we can make.

After many months out on the campaign trail, I knew parents and employers also had concerns about our schools. Parents were asking what they were getting for their tax dollars. They wondered why their children fell behind in first grade and never were able to catch up. They were frustrated because their child graduated from high school, but couldn't get into college or, if they did, they did not have foundational skills for success. Employers were worried about having a skilled workforce, and questioned why there weren't more enrollment opportunities for courses in high-demand fields, like engineering, to produce qualified graduates to fill their workforce needs.

I began talking with Judy Hartmann, my education policy adviser, about some new directions for education. Judy is a former teacher and has worked for school districts and the Washington Education Association. She would serve as my education advisor for all eight years of my time as governor.

We were convinced we couldn't provide a world-class education system simply by throwing more money at it. And while student testing was the popular trend, it didn't make much sense to test kids on coursework geared more for the previous century.

We knew we needed real reform. The question was how to get it.

I knew we couldn't get public buy-in if we simply produced another study by insiders. So we drafted a citizen-engagement plan. It was led by a 13-member steering committee and advised by 75 citizens, educators, legislators, and business and community leaders.

There was another critical element to this study. In the past, early learning, K-12 and higher education were always treated distinctly, as if they are wholly independent from each other. I was growing more convinced the "system" needed to be seamless, so three advisory committees looked at early learning, K-12 and higher education under one large umbrella.

I went to the 2005 Legislature and asked for approval of a top-to-bottom study, which would create a report we later named Washington Learns. I signed the bill into law on May 16.

To be truthful, I wasn't prepared for the size of the task we undertook. As I told one reporter when the Washington Learns report was released, "I admit I didn't appreciate the enormity and challenge of the task."

When the report was released, it received good reviews, but there were a few who complained that it didn't address the issue of school funding.

I understood the frustration, but I also felt strongly that we needed to fix the system first. It was going to be hard to get people to spend more money on schools based on the advice of a report.

For years, much of the public debate about improving schools always boiled down to reducing class size and giving schools more money.

Washington Learns concluded we needed more fundamental reforms. The study recommended five principles for change:

- Set goals for improvement in education quality, and measure ourselves against the best education systems in the nation and world;

- Tailor education to fit the needs of the individual;

- Bring creativity into the classroom;

- Engage parents, communities and private partners; and

- Commit the necessary human and financial resources to education.

I summed it up with this theme: A world-class, learner-focused, seamless education system. We needed to educate more people to higher levels.

Five initiatives were recommended to realize these principles.

The first was to invest in early learning. We found more than half the children entering kindergarten are not ready for school, and most that start behind tend to stay behind throughout their school years. These students are tomorrow's dropouts.

For us to succeed as a state and nation, we must recognize that learning begins the moment children open their eyes—they truly are born learning.

I believe the most important outcome of Washington Learns was the creation of a state Department of Early Learning. Previously, early learning programs were offered by different agencies with different missions and no coordination. For the first time, we had one agency dedicated to helping ensure there are successful early-learning programs for children who are at home, in child-care settings or in preschools, so they enter kindergarten ready to learn and ready to succeed in school.

We also created a private, non-profit organization called Thrive by Five Washington to work with the department. This was a unique, new approach. Thrive by Five can do things government can't do, like conduct demonstration projects and studies to test the most effective ways to prepare pre-school children for success in school.

Getting off to a good start is vital for kids and our communities. Research shows a great start in school helps build strong communities. For every dollar invested in quality early learning, $8 are saved through reduced need for special education and remediation, and lower rates of crime, abuse, neglect and teen pregnancy.

Washington Learns also confirmed our suspicion that in order to provide our kids with a world-class education, we need to provide a seamless learning environment from pre-school to K-12 and on through community colleges and four-year universities.

In other words, we had to stop putting pre-school, K-12 and higher education in separate silos and start planning for a seamless education system. To help kids be successful, we need to look at education from cradle to career.

Here is why the seamless concept is important. We found we were passing kids along through the school system without ensuring they were ready to succeed at the next level. The education data was discouraging. Only 74 of every 100 ninth graders, for instance, would graduate with their peers four years later.

It wasn't just kids unprepared for kindergarten. We found kids who weren't ready to progress from grade school to middle school, middle school to high school, or high school to college. When they weren't prepared, they struggled to survive at the next level.

To help ensure a smoother transition of students, we repealed the state Higher Education Coordinating Board and replaced it with the Student Achievement Council. The council has broader duties and is required to produce plans that provide smooth, seamless connections from high school through college, including community college to a four-year university.

A second initiative recognizes how vital math and science skills have become, so we began a major redesign of our math and science programs, curricula and instruction.

While it is important to set high expectations for students, we also have to realize each one is different and a cookie-cutter approach isn't effective. That's why Washington Learns moved us toward the third initiative—personalized learning programs that meet each student's skills and interests. A student who has his or her heart set on a trade should be able to focus on classes that meet that goal, and not be required to take courses designed for the college-bound.

The fourth initiative of Washington Learns laid out a road map to help ensure all students can attend college or trade schools, and that courses and training in high-demand fields are available for students.

To help educate more kids to higher levels, we brought four-year degrees closer to the students by establishing four-year programs in Tacoma, Vancouver, Bothell and the Tri-Cities.

The high cost of a college education can also be a barrier, so we created the Opportunity Scholarship Program. An Opportunity Scholarship Board, made up primarily of business leaders, will build a scholarship fund to ensure Washington's most promising young people can attend college and that our businesses have skilled, knowledgeable employees. We know we need to provide access to low-income students, but we also need to ensure middle-income students are not lost to rising tuition.

Boeing and Microsoft each contributed $25 million toward the board's goal of raising $1 billion by 2020.

In 2012, the first 3,000 students received Opportunity scholarships to pursue four-year degrees in science, technology, engineering, math and health care.

An important conclusion of the Early Learning study was to make sure our schools are producing results. Parents need to know they are getting value for their tax dollars, and we need to know if our students are graduating with educations they can count on in the job market.

Just as Washington Learns put us on a course for setting higher expectations for our children, we also needed to set a high bar for educators. I have always firmly believed that every great school has a great leader and every great classroom has a great teacher.

As our state implemented its reform measures, national-level research groups were examining other education issues. In the late spring of 2009, the Widget Report documented the shortcomings of most education evaluation systems and placed the issue squarely before educators and policy makers.

We were no exception. When I talked to Washington teachers, principals and administrators, I learned they were dissatisfied with our state's evaluation system. It had been more than two decades since it had been reviewed and clearly the content and processes were outdated.

In June 2009, I attended the Governors' Education Symposium hosted by the Hunt Institute and the National Governors' Association. Three others accompanied me: Randy Dorn, superintendent of Public Instruction; Judy Hartmann; and Mary Lindquist, president of the Washington Education Association.

Based on what we heard at the symposium, I asked Judy for more research information and ideas about how we could improve education evaluations. I engaged both Randy and Mary in months of debate and discussion.

From those talks, we asked teachers and principals to produce ideas for a new evaluation system. I was then able to convince the Legislature during the 2010 session to pass legislation that revamped the evaluation systems for teachers and principals.

In the past, all the attention was focused on teacher evaluations. Our legislation was significant in that it directed both teacher and principal evaluations be designed and implemented together so administrators and teachers are moving in the same direction in their school house. The legislation also proposed eight pilot programs so we could refine the evaluation system before taking it statewide.

Based on lessons learned from the pilots, the Legislature passed a new evaluation bill in 2012. In essence, the new evaluation got rid of broad statements of performance from the old evaluation system and replaced them with clear descriptors of what it takes to be a successful teacher.

As I said when I signed the legislation, "The old system just didn't work. It was too broad and didn't really help anybody. For the first time, Washington public school teachers and principals will know exactly what is required of them." They will continually grow.

Looking back on our work to overhaul evaluations, I realized Mary was the only representative from a teachers' union at the National Governors' Association meeting—and the only one ever to be invited to attend the Governors' Symposium. This is important to note because it helps explain the level of success states have had, or failed to achieve, in designing and implementing new evaluation systems.

In Washington, we involved teachers and principals from the beginning, and the combination of on-the-ground expertise and quality research resulted in meaningful, new evaluation systems.

Throughout my governorship, the need for additional funding for K-12 education has been a continual concern. This was an area in which Washington Learns gathered a lot of data, but was not able to fully develop recommendations. A group was created to examine this topic. Their recommendations to the Legislature and subsequent deliberations resulted in two pieces of legislation that set forth targets and a phase-in plan for basic-education funding.

What has made funding so hard to implement? The public needs to believe that additional funds will result in better student outcomes; that we know where and how to spend it; and that the outcomes will be seen by our students, parents and citizens.

In 2012, the State Supreme Court ruled the Legislature must make progress on funding basic education. As I develop my final state budget, I will ask for a significant down payment in the 2013-2015 biennium. By 2018, the state will need to spend $1.6 billion more per year on K-12 education alone. That is a significant challenge for the Legislature and taxpayers.

I believe that the education system has made great progress toward reform, but the resources to complete the work still must come. This is the other half of the bargain. Our high expectations for students, educators and schools must be matched by citizen and voter support for the funds to make them real.

Bridgeport has demonstrated what can be achieved with high expectations. If you want another example, then travel to Bremerton where the Washington National Guard and educators are doing remarkable things for kids who desperately need a second chance.

Tucked in with the Guard's Readiness Center is the Washington Youth Academy. The academy provides an intervention program for youths 16 to 18 years old and who are at risk of dropping out or have dropped out of high school.

The academy offers a quasi-military setting where an academic and mentoring program improves life skills, raises education levels and increases employment potential.

It's a tough program for those who enroll, and based on the Academy's remarkable record of success, there is no shortage of applicants for the 22-week program.

"It is a tough-love approach. We don't allow excuses and we expect them to meet standards," explains Colonel Larry Pierce, the academy's director.

"Many of the kids are held to discipline standards for the first time in their lives," he added. Each class has about 150 students, and on average 120 graduate.

Lynn Caddell worked in public schools before coming to the academy. "Everyone talks about increasing a student's self esteem so they can achieve. We are teaching them how to achieve so it will increase self esteem," she said.

"When you get kids doing what they didn't think they could do, like rappelling off a 60-foot tower or finally doing long-division, you begin building self esteem," Pierce added. "Kids are with us 24 hours a day and we don't allow quitting."

After their five months at the Academy, most students leave with a significant increase in academic growth and high school credits. All are expected to go back to school and work with a mentor who serves as a role model and helps guide them to graduation.

Congressman Norm Dicks had heard about similar Guard academies in other parts of the country and urged me to start a program here.

Working with Major General Tim Lowenberg, my head of the National Guard, I was able to get the Legislature to approve $5 million in start-up money and convinced Bremerton Schools Superintendent Bette Hyde to sponsor the program. Bette later became my director of the Early Learning Department.

"I remember at ground breaking, the Governor looked at me and said, 'I used a lot of political capital to get this program,'" Caddell recalls. "I remember thinking: I believe she just told me not to screw this up."

I am pleased to say they did not "screw it up" and hundreds of young adults have successfully turned their lives around thanks to a second chance and high expectations.

I am sure mom would have approved.

Studied to Death

MAKING DECISIONS ON TRANSPORTATION MEGAPROJECTS

SOMETIMES meetings on hard-fought policy matters have strange outcomes.

Consider, for instance, the afternoon spent with a roomful of state Department of Transportation engineers and Jennifer Ziegler, my transportation advisor.

My goal was to make a final decision about the Alaskan Way Viaduct along the Seattle waterfront.

The viaduct has been a fixture—some would say eyesore—for nearly six decades. While the elevated highway leaves a two-mile-long gray scar along the western face of Seattle, it also is a vital transportation link that carries 20 to 25 percent of the north-south traffic through downtown.

For a number of years, engineers worried about whether the viaduct had reached the end of its useful life. Then Mother Nature stepped in. On Feb. 28, 2001, the magnitude-6.8 Nisqually earthquake rattled the Puget Sound region. Engineers later said that if the quake had lasted just a little longer, the viaduct could have been flattened with the potential of a horrible loss of life, monumental traffic problems and significant economic impacts on Seattle and the state.

Inspections after the quake confirmed what everyone knew—there was extensive damage to the aging structure's joints and columns.

Even before the earthquake, discussions about replacing the viaduct dated as far back as 1995. And roughly 14 years later (eight years after the Nisqually quake) I was anxious to make a decision and move forward.

There had been numerous studies about various options. Downtown

29

business owners, labor, environmentalists, commuters, freight haulers, port officials, local elected officials and many more people had waded into the debate.

I was ready to make a decision, but I decided to poll the roomful of staffers first. Half the engineers voted for what was called the "cut and cover" option and the other half voted for a surface option. Jennifer, a non-engineer, said she couldn't decide.

"How am I supposed to make a decision when half my staff votes for one option, the other half votes for the other, and my policy person is undecided?" I asked.

Months later, when Jennifer and I reminisced about the meeting, she grinned and said, "I went home that night and decided to take up running." She did indeed take up running. Years later she was still at it and had even run in a few marathons.

The viaduct debates and a similar fight over another megaproject just a few miles away—the State Route 520 bridge replacement over Lake Washington—offer interesting lessons in making decisions about major transportation projects. They're highly controversial, cost taxpayers billions of dollars, leave a lasting footprint on our cities, affect lifestyles and have profound effects on our economy.

Because of the high stakes involved in megaprojects, you have to be careful or they will be studied and processed to death. Obviously there has to be study and public involvement, but we were spending time and money on the viaduct and highway 520 that we couldn't afford.

The 520 project involved a highly vulnerable, but vital traffic corridor. For years, engineers had been warning us that sustained windstorms with gusts greater than 50 mph could break or crack the drawspan, anchor cables or pontoons, and cause the bridge to sink. An earthquake could also result in catastrophic failure. The Department of Transportation began analyzing options for replacing the vulnerable bridge in 1997 and completed the final environmental impact statement in 2011—that's 14 years of process before any construction started.

Meanwhile, interest groups were passionate about what kind of project they wanted. Residents on the east side of Lake Washington wanted an eight-lane bridge to help move traffic and commerce swiftly across the bridge. Residential owners on the west side wanted a smaller footprint, like the current, four-lane bridge, which wouldn't mar the beauty of the lake or disrupt the west side. Environmentalists, meanwhile, also argued for a smaller bridge, stating that if you add more lanes you promote sprawl and more reliance on cars and fossil fuels.

There were battles over the options for replacing the viaduct as well: a surface street, another elevated roadway, or a tunnel.

After multiple environmental studies, public votes and shifting political winds (as administrations changed in Seattle), I decided we had to make a decision and move on. "There isn't a good time to make a decision. You either do it or we're forced watch the viaduct pancake and the 520 bridge sink," I told one reporter.

I brought all the parties together to force a decision on the viaduct. Now, to be truthful, this particular decision benefited greatly from timely advancement in construction techniques. We learned that a deep-bore tunnel had been successfully built in Spain. It proved we could build a single, large-diameter tunnel at far less cost than the double-bore tunnel, which had been studied before.

As a result, we were able to get agreement among the mayor of Seattle, the King County executive and director of the Port of Seattle on the single, large-diameter, bored-tunnel option, which included two lanes of traffic in each direction. The tunnel could be constructed without disrupting traffic for years on the viaduct. And it gave the city the ability to plan for a spectacular new waterfront.

We used a similar community process for the 520 bridge, and on May 13, 2009, I signed a bill that would fund a new 520 bridge with two lanes in each direction and two new carpool lanes. The design would lead to a bridge that could withstand high winds and an earthquake.

There is another important lesson underlying decision-making for transportation megaprojects. I made decisions about the viaduct and 520 in late

2008 and 2009. Just three or four years earlier, I wouldn't have been able to make those calls.

That's because the Department of Transportation was not a cabinet agency under the authority of the governor. It was run by a seven-member commission appointed by the governor.

The commission form of governance had been in place for years. Many viewed it as a safeguard against political patronage. The old system was also viewed as less political in the larger sense, allowing transportation secretaries to remain on the job while governors came and went. In reality, though, the average length of service for transportation secretaries in the United States is about two-and-a-half years, which makes it harder to have steady, long-term leadership.

There are downsides to commission governance, though. It is hard to get decisive leadership as there are seven bosses instead of one. Accountability is hard with seven non-elected, volunteer commissioners. A governor has to answer directly to the public every four years.

As a brand-new governor, I quickly learned that the public held me accountable for transportation even though I didn't hire the secretary, nor approve budgets or the statewide transportation plan. So long as I was getting blamed for transportation issues, I figured I might as well have the authority.

Therefore, I didn't object when, in my first legislative session, legislators approved a bill placing transportation under my authority.

As I saw responsibility for the agency coming my way, I decided that if I was going to be accountable, I should have the flexibility to deliver results and fix problems. So I supported a proposal for a new gas tax.

Supporters told me I was crazy, that if I survived the ongoing court challenge to my narrow-election victory, I would never get re-elected with the tax hike hanging around my neck.

I was convinced, however, that if we could show legislators and the public exactly what we would build with the money and that we would be held accountable to deliver the projects on time and on budget, we would get support.

It wasn't easy. I worked on an eleventh-hour turnaround after the gas tax bill failed in the House the day before the end of session. Aided by business, which knew we needed better roads to get workers to work and freight to market, the Transportation Partnership Act (TPA) passed the last day of session.

The TPA raised the price of gas by 9.5 cents per gallon over four years and, combined with an earlier 5-cent per gallon tax, provided the state with $16.3 billion in transportation projects. It was the biggest transportation construction initiative in state history. Money for the 520 bridge and the viaduct was included.

As expected, an initiative was filed asking voters in November to repeal the gas tax. Initiative supporters gathered more than 420,000 signatures to get the initiative on the ballot and predicted that the gas tax would be wiped out at the polls.

Thanks to a strong anti-initiative vote in King and Snohomish counties, voters supported the new gas tax. I am convinced it was because we were able to explain, at a very personal level, exactly what the tax would buy and demonstrate why the tax was needed to improve safety, reduce commute times and provide a highway system needed for business growth.

It is one thing to tell people what they will get for their money. It is another to deliver on that promise. Our Department of Transportation, under Secretary Doug MacDonald, reported back to me regularly through our Government Management Accountability Program and maintained an on-time, on-budget record of nearly 90 percent.

Following Doug's retirement in the summer of 2007, I selected Paula Hammond as secretary in October. She is an engineer, a long-time employee of the agency and their first female secretary. In total, 88 percent of the projects were completed early or on time, and 91 percent were completed on or under budget. By the end of 2012, 370 of the total 421 projects were completed or under way.

The failed 2005 anti-gas tax initiative wasn't the first attempt to influence transportation policy in Washington. In 1999, voters approved Initiative

695 to roll back motor vehicle excise taxes, which paid for a wide variety of services, including ferries.

The action left the ferry system critically underfunded, with operating costs for fuel and labor outpacing fare-box revenue. As a result, ferry and terminal preservation work were delayed, and funds that should have been budgeted for highway work were diverted to keep ferries afloat.

The department tried to do the usual: make do by patching together service and applying Band-Aids to problems in an attempt to shield the public from the true impact of the vote.

It all came to a head with a phone call I received from Paula just before Thanksgiving weekend in 2007.

It was within weeks of Paula's appointment as secretary. She told me the state's four Steel Electric class ferries that were built in 1927 had cracks in their hulls. She wanted to pull them out of the water and from service immediately.

Actually, typical of straight-talking Paula, she said she wasn't asking me if she could pull them out of service, she was telling me she had to. She said the cracks looked like spider webs in the single-hull vessels. I was glad Paula was an engineer who recognized the risk to public safety and had the courage to make a call that was bold but correct.

The action, however, left the Port Townsend-Keystone run without a ferry right before the Thanksgiving holiday rush.

Paula and her staff scrambled to patch together temporary service that would last until new ferries were built in 2010.

One real lesson from all of this is that government has to better manage the initiative process. Initiatives mandate expensive new services—like smaller class sizes in schools—without providing the funds to pay for it. Or they cut taxes, like the motor vehicle excise tax, without identifying how the cuts will be made and to what services. Public expectations from initiatives are not aligned with budget realities.

Despite the transportation progress made in recent years, there is much left to do. In 2011, I convened the Connecting Washington Task Force to develop a sustainable, 10-year investment and revenue strategy for the state's transportation system. The task force identified $50 billion in unmet transportation needs at the state and local level over the next 10 years. For instance, the northbound lanes of the Columbia River Crossing were built in 1917 for horse and buggy travel. Today, 135,000 vehicles cross the Columbia River and spend a significant amount of time (upwards of six hours every day) fighting through congestion and delays. The bridge sorely needs more capacity.

Improvements for Washington's economic competitiveness also are still necessary on I-5, I-405 and I-90 across Snoqualmie Pass. Our container ports desperately require the completion of highways 509 and 167.

In addition to investments in key economic corridors, we need to develop a dedicated source of funding for operating and maintaining Washington's transportation system. Because the 5-cent and TPA gas taxes did not provide maintenance or preservation funds for state and local roads or our ferry system, deterioration will set over time.

Our transportation system touches every aspect of our lives. We take it for granted that it will deliver the food we eat. We expect it to get us to work and take our products to market. Because people use the system constantly, they feel like transportation experts and have high expectations for our ferries and roadways. Transportation policy is going to be a big challenge well into the future. It will take backbone to make tough decisions on megaprojects. It also will require a major effort to figure out how to pay for and maintain a safe, effective transportation system.

Take Two Aspirin

MY STAFF AND CABINET see to it that I don't get much time to read books of my choice. I go home each night to a foot-high pile of briefing papers, reports, emails, articles and briefs for the next day's events.

Within months of taking office, Steve Hill, my director of the Health Care Authority, gave me a copy of *Epidemic of Care* by George C. Halvorson, George J. Isham, M.D., and others. It had a profound influence on my views about health care reform.

The book's basic theme is that far too much health care in the United States today is given with little or no regard to whether it works.

For example, 135 doctors were asked to prescribe a treatment for one specific diagnosed condition for a specific patient. The doctors came up with 82 different treatments. The myriad of treatments happened for a variety of reasons. Maybe the doctor was working from information provided by her drug sales rep. Perhaps his training was old and he wasn't aware of recent recommended best practices.

Epidemic of Care hit home with me because, as a relatively new governor, I was astounded at the huge health care costs facing state government and the staggering growth of those costs each year.

Of the many costs borne by state government, none have been as vexing as those paid for health care. Today, Washington state spends $5 billion on health care every year. The majority of that is care for low-income and vulnerable people, which, as a share of the General Fund, has doubled over the past two decades from 7 percent in 1991 to 15 percent in 2012.

During the past two decades, health care costs increased dramatically for Washington's largest employers, including the state. Washington state is not unique: Nationally, health care costs are projected to account for almost 20 percent of the Gross Domestic Product—that's $1 of every $5 spent in the United States. These out-of-control costs take funds away from other needs, like the state's ability to pay for education.

Costs were soaring when I took office. It would have been one thing if more patients were getting high-quality care, I told myself. In reality, though, we had neither broader coverage nor better quality to justify the escalating costs.

In 2004, I learned the uninsured population expanded by 11 percent to 603,000 citizens, including more than 96,000 kids. It wasn't just the very-poor or near-poor who were without coverage. Costs were rising so fast that the middle class was without coverage, too.

Data on the quality of care were also disturbing. According to some reports, 20 to 30 percent of health care spending did not improve health or extend life. Another study concluded that each year between 39,000 and 83,000 deaths nationally resulted from preventable medical errors.

The more I learned, the more frustrated I became. As governor, I saw we were paying more and more for a health care system that had too much waste, too many errors and too much unproven or ineffective treatment.

For instance, Dr. Don Berwick, a former Medicaid/Medicare director for the Obama administration, estimated the waste in our health care system in 2011 was as much as $1.3 trillion.

Another study, by the U.S. Office of Inspector General in 2011, found 293 errors in a review of 785 patient records. The hospitals reported only 40 of those errors, and only reported two of the 18 errors that led to permanent disability or death.

I soon discovered that finding problems with our health care system was much easier than coming up with solutions. Like a lot of things, health care politics are about money—a lot of money—and when you talk about reform, it means someone's billfold is threatened and he or she will put up resistance.

I also found health care reform can be like the game Whac-A-Mole.

Every time we would try to make a change, there could be unforeseen consequences, requiring even more change.

What I found most difficult of all, though, was the partisanship and myths about health care. For instance, I heard constantly that individual mandates, which require insurers to pay for specific coverage, boost costs. Yet when I asked experts from the insurance carriers if it would reduce costs if we eliminated mandates, such as prostate cancer screening or reconstructive surgery after a mastectomy—the answer was no.

Sometimes, when working on volatile public policy issues with a long history, you have to try to wipe the slate clean, start from ground zero, and trust your own curiosity to find common ground and new directions.

I knew it would be a slow, tedious and painful process, and I also knew I needed legislators to take the journey with me. So I decided to work with legislators on a Blue Ribbon Commission on Health Care Costs and Access. I remember realizing it wasn't going to be an easy task when I heard that one Republican member said his sole purpose for being on the commission was "to make sure Gregoire doesn't have any successes."

Later, a Democratic state representative stopped me and asked if we would get a party-line outcome from the commission. "I don't know," I told him. He was puzzled and a bit chagrined when I told him I hoped the commission would engage in "learning beyond the rhetoric."

Fortunately, we did move beyond the rhetoric, and our bipartisan group agreed on key goals that, over the next few years, paved the way for significant reforms in the delivery of health care. One goal was to provide more access to care. Second, we wanted to make care more affordable by reducing waste and introducing systemic changes with health information technology and electronic health records. We also wanted to improve the health of Washingtonians by emphasizing wellness, health promotion and prevention. Finally, we were committed to improving quality by increasing the use of evidence-based practices.

When it came to expanding coverage, I was convinced the most urgent need was to provide coverage for more children. Our kids have enough challenges to succeed in school and life, so I wanted to make sure we offered them every chance for a healthy start.

To expand coverage, I proposed making more kids eligible for public health care. We created a new program called Apple Health for Kids, and, in my early budgets, we increased funding to provide coverage for 100,000 more children. By 2012, nearly all children in Washington had access to care. Providing a healthy start for kids was so important to me that I insisted on maintaining funding for the program even through the deepest budget cuts. Our Legislature was very supportive. This was one of my proudest accomplishments.

When it came to getting more value for our health care dollars, I realized I would have far more ability to make changes in health care practices if I first focused on the state health care systems. The state provides health care coverage to about 1.3 million people through Medicaid, which serves low-income individuals; the state workforce; inmates at the Department of Corrections; and the workers' compensation system at the Department of Labor and Industries.

Not only did I have more influence over these systems, but they represented a rich market to test our reform ideas.

Our first initiative was to make Washington one of the first states to use scientific evidence in health care purchasing decisions.

There is no question that innovations in medicine have improved the health and lives of patients. But too often new products and treatments are introduced, at great cost, without independent, scientific evidence showing they are safe, effective, better than existing treatments and bring good outcomes for patients.

An example of our success was the first-of-its-kind Health Technology Assessment Program. Basically, we pay for new treatments or equipment only if we know they are safe and benefit the patient.

Here is an example: Traditionally, MRIs have been done with the patient lying down. Then a company devised a stand-up MRI. The trouble is the new machine and tests cost up to six times more than regular MRIs and there is zero evidence they are more effective. After a thorough review and decision by the program's clinical committee, composed of practicing physicians, we decided not to cover them. Today, decisions by the Health Technology Assessment Program are saving the state an estimated $31 million a year, but more importantly are providing only high-quality, proven care.

In the past, all the state systems purchased health care separately. To increase efficiency and the state's purchasing power, we merged the Medicaid and state employee health systems. It was one of the biggest reforms in state government in decades.

Doug Porter headed this merger. Thanks to his leadership and reforms like the one that allows bulk purchasing of prescription drugs, Washington's Medicaid costs are now among the lowest in the country, running below 2 percent annual inflation.

Another area we committed to was providing long-term care in home and community-based settings instead of more expensive institutional settings. An 80-year-old woman who may need some help during the day with medications and getting dressed has a far better quality of life by staying in her home instead of moving into an expensive nursing home.

I also am proud of an agreement we brokered with Kathleen Sebelius, U.S. Health and Human Services secretary, to offer better-coordinated care to patients who are called dual eligibles. These are individuals who often are elderly, seriously disabled and vulnerable to the extent they are eligible for Medicare and Medicaid. The agreement will streamline care for these patients, who are often in and out of the hospital and nursing homes.

It wasn't enough to just change state government's delivery of health care. We decided to branch out and work with the external market, too. We found a lot of good practices in the private sector, but because there were no efforts to take them to scale, I asked Steve Hill to look for ways to work with the private sector to cut costs and improve the quality of care.

Steve is a retired Weyerhaeuser executive who has helped spur innovation in our state retirement and health care programs. He also is chairperson of the Puget Sound Health Alliance.

One of his projects involved working in partnership with public and private employers. This included the chronic-care initiative that was led by Boeing, and the Dr. Robert Bree Collaborative to identify unnecessary variations in health care.

Steve helped expand the pioneering work by Boeing. Nationally, about 5 percent of patients represent 50 percent of health care costs. Boeing found that by providing more intensive treatment to these patients, they could greatly cut costs. Under Steve's leadership, we brought other employers together to implement Boeing's model that uses clinic-based nurses to check in with patients to see how they're doing or if they need help, and a redesigned payment system to save time and money and compensate providers fairly. Boeing found significant savings and great employee/patient satisfaction.

This is a good example of a successful multi-purchaser campaign to change health care. But it also demonstrated how hard it is to scale-up a good idea on a statewide basis. Even though the effort started with many private and public employers around the table, after more than a year of work, only employers who used the same single insurer agreed to cooperatively continue the effort and scale-up Boeing's cost-saving idea.

The good news is the state, Boeing and other large employers, like Alaska Airlines and King County, are moving forward to not only implement this great idea statewide, but also provide better-quality care to their employees. Other positive news out of this effort is the provider groups across the state are now on board, and many others are interested. Their efforts became the foundation for a major federal grant application that my team put together for statewide health care system and payment reform. A decision is expected soon.

The Bree Collaborative is the next generation in health care problem solving for our state. The Collaborative is a group of people, including doctors, hospitals, employers, insurance plan executives and state agency medical directors, chaired by Steve. This data-driven initiative looks for wide variations in certain treatments or practices and then uses a group of clinicians and health care experts to recommend evidence-based strategies for improving outcomes and reducing costs for the patient.

The decisions are then mandates for the state payers, with the idea that private payers will also be more likely to use ideas in their business models. The Bree Collaborative brings high-quality care to the forefront and encourages the market to incent and replicate these best practices for everyone across the state.

One early focus for the collaborative, for instance, was obstetric practices. The state pays for about half of the births in Washington, so I wanted to make sure we were doing all we can to tamp down costs and drive quality.

In its studies, the collaborative found major variability in the use of inductions, C-sections and vaginal births at hospitals across the state. In the Yakima Valley Memorial and Othello hospitals, for instance, elective C-section rates are less than 3 percent and dropping, while at other hospitals that rate is as high as 30 percent. Those figures raise serious questions about the quality of care that new moms and their babies are getting.

One of my last initiatives as governor was highlighting this report at the state's obstetrics conference, where hundreds of physicians convene. I talked about the need to reduce this variation and provide the best care for mothers and babies. I partnered with organizations such as the March of Dimes and the Washington State Hospital Association to make sure the word got out. Both groups have done wonderful work to reduce prematurity by raising awareness and the quality of care.

My Secretary of Health, Mary Selecky, frequently reminded me that prevention is always the best first step in reducing health care costs. "Health is wealth. Let's invest where there's a return," she stresses.

Mary came to Olympia in 1999 as Gov. Gary Locke's health secretary. She had served for 20 years as administrator of the Northeast Tri-County Health District in Colville. Reflecting her roots in rural Northeast Washington, Mary is candid, direct and passionate about public health.

Mary points out that our existing health care system consumes 96 cents out of every health care dollar for medical care. Research, however, shows medical care is only 10 percent of what influences how healthy we are. More important to our health is our family history, how healthy our environment is, and our personal lifestyle choices, like exercise, nutrition and tobacco use. Despite these findings, funding to influence these factors comprise only a fraction of our health care spending.

To reverse this trend, Mary urged me to sign an executive order to use our influence, as a purchaser of health care services for 1.3 million people, to include performance measures in state health contracts. By doing so, we foster healthy outcomes through such things as better vaccination rates, smoking cessation programs and more physical activity.

As attorney general, I sued tobacco companies in the 1990s, partly due to evidence they were targeting kids to make them the next generation of smokers. In our settlement with tobacco companies, which was the largest financial settlement ever, I obtained funding to discourage the use of tobacco.

This prevention initiative was right in Mary's wheelhouse. When Mary took on the challenge, Washington was 20th in the nation in tobacco use— nearly one in four adults were smoking. Mary didn't tiptoe into the campaign. She borrowed an ad from California featuring a woman named Debi, who, as a result of smoking as a young teen, developed cancer of the larynx. In the ad, she smoked through a hole in her throat, called a stoma, which was the result of her cancer surgery.

To this day, people still talk about the Debi ads and the graphic way they told the story of how addictive and ruinous tobacco use is to your health.

The Debi ad and other campaign measures worked. Youth smoking in Washington is down by nearly half since 2000 and adult smoking dropped by 30 percent. For every dollar we spend on tobacco prevention, Mary always reminds me, $5 is saved in future health care costs.

Mary and I shared another passion—health care for kids. One of the most important steps we can take to protect kids from preventable diseases is immunizations. I will never forget the first time Mary emphatically told me about the need for immunizations and thoughtful public health planning for horrible events like a possible contagion or epidemic: "Remember, Governor…Bugs rule…Bugs rule!"

We have experienced two serious events: a scare of H1N1 (swine flu) and a full-blown epidemic of pertussis (whooping cough). These awful bugs rule indeed. Whooping cough can be serious for infants who often must be hospitalized because they have not been fully immunized, which does not occur until they get older, and because their small lungs can't handle the dangerous coughing fits, which can suffocate them.

Dramatic state budget cuts triggered by the recession threatened our efforts to immunize all children. To solve the problem, Mary worked with members of the Legislature, especially Rep. Eileen Cody, to create a non-profit organization to make sure we could carry on our immunization work. Washington has risen from 45th to 16th in the nation today in immunization rates.

While we were successful in expanding coverage, eliminating waste and improving quality, it was clear that if we wanted comprehensive changes to health care, we needed the federal government to step up and pass reform legislation.

The politically charged Patient Protection and Affordable Care Act, or ACA, provided that reform. I was pleased to see that it incorporated many of the ideas we had put in place. With partisan politics raging around the law, some governors vowed to block implementation in their states.

Not me.

I saw a chance to get health care services to thousands of Washington residents who needed help: like people with pre-existing conditions who needed coverage; uninsured young adults not covered on their parents' policies; and 350,000 people eligible for an expanded Medicaid program.

I moved quickly to begin implementing the act. I used an executive order to create a Health Care Cabinet, and named Jonathan Seib, my health care policy advisor, to coordinate the team.

I convinced lawmakers to pass legislation creating a centerpiece of the ACA—the Washington's Health Benefit Exchange, a Web-based marketplace for buyers and consumers of health coverage. I signed that law on the second anniversary of the ACA.

I set a goal to reduce medical inflation to between 4 and 5 percent across the board in Washington. I knew employers were being crushed with ever-ratcheting health care costs and the stability of the state budget called for it.

Even though no one thought it would happen in the timeline I set, amazingly it has: Our Medicaid costs are lower than 2 percent. The Department of Labor and Industries, Department of Corrections and our state employee programs have all performed well. In fact, *The New England Journal of Medicine*, one of the nation's most respected medical journals, published an article in 2012 about how states' health care costs for employers have stabilized. This is due to several factors, including reforms; the spotlight on health care costs; and systemic changes, like the ACA, health information technology and the things we've accomplished in Washington state.

I doubt Steve realized what he was starting when he handed me *Epidemic of Care* seven years ago. I'd like to think that it provided me with the insights to steer clear of the partisanship surrounding health care and instead ask the questions that helped us slash through waste and boost quality.

We still have a long ways to go, but we are off to a solid start.

Water is for Fighting

ENDING THE WATER WARS IN WASHINGTON

ONE WARM, fall morning I stood on the banks of the Walla Walla River and watched as a salmon slowly worked its way upstream.

It wasn't any ordinary salmon.

It was one of the first spring Chinook salmon to swim this section of river in more than a century! As we cheered the arrival of a fish run extinct for so many years, I noticed tears in the eyes of several of my tribal colleagues.

For centuries, abundant salmon runs in the Walla Walla sustained Native Americans. Then settlers began diverting the river for agriculture, and new water channels were installed to prevent periodic flooding of local towns. The river actually dried up at certain times of the year. Until now, that is.

Tribes, irrigators, farmers, cities, conservationists and others teamed up to restore the Walla Walla flows and salmon runs.

The return of an extinct salmon run to the Walla Walla River is just one sign of progress made in ending decades of water wars in Eastern Washington. It is a story of getting bitter antagonists to trust each other, cooperate and work toward common goals.

Most people would find it inconceivable that there is not enough water to go around in Washington state. After all, it rains more than 150 days a year in Seattle, and there's water everywhere you look.

Especially in arid Eastern Washington, even with the mighty Columbia River, the demand to make water available for fish, farms, families and businesses has exceeded supply for decades.

Water wars are so bitter and long-lasting that Mark Twain deadpanned,

"Whiskey is for drinking, water is for fighting."

The fight over water has raged in Eastern Washington for more than 40 years. I began working on water issues back in 1988 as director of the Department of Ecology. I quickly learned how high emotions can run when it comes to water—I was hung in effigy in the Methow Valley over an issue involving water rights.

In Washington, like other portions of the West, water is an economic engine. A reliable source of water is absolutely crucial to our $2.5 billion agricultural industry. When I traveled abroad to tout our agricultural products, I visited countries where every french fry is imported from Washington state. In 2011, our potato exports were worth almost $700 million in just Asia. The potato industry alone supports 25,000 people. We export our apples, cherries and world-class wine, whose industry provides another 30,000 jobs.

It didn't take long for water issues to land in my lap as governor. Less than two months after taking office, I traveled to the banks of the Yakima River and declared a statewide drought emergency. Across Washington, precipitation was at or near record lows, and the snowpack, critical to water supplies over the summer, was at just 26 percent of normal.

The drought hit irrigators particularly hard. There are hundreds of Eastern Washington farmers whose water rights can be cut off in low-water years, which can spell ruin for their crops and livelihoods. Even the city of Roslyn has a "junior" water right that can be cut off in water-short years.

But droughts are just part of the problem. In the Odessa region, there are more than 100,000 acres of rich farmland irrigated by groundwater. Farmers, however, are pumping water faster than the aquifers can recharge. Water levels have dropped so precipitously that some wells today are as deep as 2,400 feet and the water is hot and concentrated with sodium.

Odessa is the heartland of potato growing. Farmers and processors feed french fries to the world, and if the aquifer drops to a level where the wells can no longer be used, Washington could lose $1.6 billion in farm income.

Meanwhile, cities have been unable to get a water right, which has stymied growth and development of new businesses. Salmon have lost habitat and stream flows, causing their numbers to decline.

With so much at stake, you would think the parties would work together to find a solution. But the fighting raged on for years and produced not a drop of new water.

The drought and declining aquifer levels convinced me we couldn't afford to continue the decades-long stalemate. So I called in Jay Manning, my director of Ecology. Jay had been my lead counsel from the Attorney General's Office while I was at Ecology. He had worked with me on a number of sensitive negotiations, including the Tri-Party Agreement to clean up the Hanford Reservation.

We knew we had to get past the long-standing attitudes about water legislation being a zero-sum game—where there would be only winners or losers. We had to convince people they could win, but they would have to give up something in the process.

Our other strategy was to encourage a bottom-up approach. I was convinced a solution forced on people from Olympia wouldn't work. We needed real problem solving from the stakeholders.

Water legislation had emerged in the 2005 session, but it was clear there were still deep differences and little chance of passage. I have learned that sometimes, when there are sharp divisions and little progress being made on legislation, it helps to relieve the pressure and try for a fresh start. So I asked legislators to step back and make a new run at the issue after session.

"The governor was willing to set aside the past to bring life for the future," one of my policy advisors, Keith Phillips, recalls.

We formed a work group with representatives from each of the caucuses in the House and Senate, along with my staff. When I convened the group, I told them the fighting had gone on long enough. Years of contention had not produced a drop of water. I urged them to take a new approach, this time with the recognition we could meet the needs of all, but only if everyone agreed to give some.

The group spent the interim holding hearings around the state, and while they made some progress, they never were able to get stakeholders to rally around a bill. Frustrated by the lack of progress, Senator Bob Morton, a Republican from Kettle Falls, and Senator Erik Paulsen, a Democrat from West Seattle, agreed to have stakeholders meet in a room and not come out until they had reached an agreement.

For the first time, there was a discussion about providing something for everyone. But we still weren't out of the woods. Legislators were worried that they could not get enough votes to pass the bill.

Compounding the problem was the fact that there was no money to pay for the bill. Many legislators felt they would be asked to take a tough vote with no assurances anything would ever be accomplished.

During a Saturday morning meeting with legislators, I announced I was prepared to put $200 million into the capital budget to pay for water projects. The state funds would leverage even more in federal money. By raising the stakes, I was hoping to convince them that I was committed—that this time it was real and to galvanize action. And it worked. On Feb. 16, 2006, I signed the Columbia River management bill.

"Twenty-five years we have worked to break this logjam," I said at the bill signing. "Environmentalists, farmers, tribal governments, fish managers, cities and towns: They all did their homework and were heard."

The key was getting people to work together. They realized that if they didn't work together, they would walk away with nothing. But if they help, everyone gets some piece of the pie, and they will get their share.

The bill I signed fundamentally changes the way we manage water. The idea is to manage this natural resource in a smarter way and give all users a portion of the new water. We basically wanted to capture some of the heavy spring flows and release it at times most beneficial to farmers and fish. The state's $200 million, along with money from the federal government and farmers, will provide storage for the water and fund conservation projects to reduce the loss of irrigation water to evaporation and seepage into the canal soil.

The bill also provided a new formula for new water distribution. Two-thirds goes to out-of-stream use while one-third goes to in-stream flows

and fish. The Department of Ecology was tasked with aggressively developing new water supplies through storage, conservation and the creation of
markets where people can buy or sell water rights, including the purchase
of water for fish runs.

It took agreement by strange bedfellows to pass the Columbia River bill.
But what is encouraging is that the spirit of cooperation is spreading.

In August 2012, a new plan to provide water for fish, families and farms
was unveiled for the Yakima basin. Here is how four conservation group
leaders described the plan in *Crosscut*, a Seattle online newspaper: "It's a
precedent-setting opportunity to restore salmon, protect public lands and
rivers, increase the reliability of water supplies for farmers and create more
jobs in the basin."

They acknowledged there are parts of the plan they don't like, such as
building new dams, expanding reservoirs and flooding some old-growth
forests. But in exchange, they get salmon recovery, habitat restoration, wa-
ter-quality improvements, and new wilderness and wild-and-scenic river
designations.

As they so articulately wrote: "It will bring back what may be the largest
sockeye run on the West Coast, protect more of this gorgeous landscape
with one pen stroke than we've been able to save in the last 28 years, and
make peace in one of the longest-running water conflicts in the West."

It was music to my ears to have Harry Smiskin, the chairman of the
Confederated Tribes of the Yakama Indian Nation, say at one of the group
meetings, "The time for conflict is over. It's time for us to go work to get
something done."

Not a bad outcome considering the previous 40-year drought on water
policy. And it all came about because people were finally willing to put aside
their differences and work for real solutions.

Troubled Waters

THE CHALLENGE OF CLEANING UP PUGET SOUND

ON A RAINY, winter day, trillions of fecal coliform bacteria are washed from fields and yards into the streams and rivers feeding beautiful Samish Bay.

The bacteria come from faulty septic systems, dairy farms, livestock, wildlife, recreational users and even pets. When the levels are too high, the state Department of Health closes shellfish harvesting and recreational use on the bay.

The closures are not a rare occurrence. In 2012, pollution closed the bay for 60 days. Hardest hit is the Samish's $3 million-a-year shellfish industry. Oyster growers have to stop their harvest, which means they not only lose sales, they are unable to meet customer expectations for dependable deliveries. Workers are laid off until the beaches are reopened, and consumer confidence in the quality of shellfish suffers.

Bill Dewey, who manages public affairs for Taylor Shellfish Farms, knows how discouraging closures can be for growers. When the Samish is closed, Taylor can use its shellfish farms on other bays to fill customer orders. Other growers, with operations only on the Samish, aren't so lucky. They are shut down for the duration of the closure.

The Samish isn't unique. It is just one example of the continuing pressure Puget Sound faces from pollution and our challenge to clean it up.

Over the past 20 years, three agencies with three separate approaches have attempted to restore the iconic jewel of Washington. The Puget Sound Partnership, the latest agency to lead the massive cleanup effort, has not had the success I had hoped for. The agency's 2012 State of the Sound report concludes we have slowed the decline in health of Puget Sound, but the region is still losing ground in many measures.

We aren't alone. A report by the U.S. Government Accountability Office (GAO) found that agencies trying to clean up the nation's other great and vital estuaries, including Chesapeake Bay, the Everglades and Great Lakes, also are struggling.

Despite the huge challenges and mixed results so far, I have not given up on a goal of making Puget Sound open for fishing, swimming and shellfish digging by 2020.

We don't have a choice. A strong Washington economy is impossible without a healthy, vibrant Puget Sound. About 70 percent of all jobs and 77 percent of the total income in the state comes from the Puget Sound basin. Tourism, fishing, commercial shellfish harvesting and other marine industries survive only with a clean, healthy Sound.

As I leave office, I believe the cleanup is on the right track, but I also recognize we are entering a new and sensitive phase that will be politically charged and introduce new challenges.

Long gone are the days when we thought the solution to pollution was to simply stop toxic discharges from the ends of industrial pipes.

Puget Sound, the second-largest estuary in the United States, is fed by 10,000 rivers and streams. We now know we have to address human pollution sources from all the land that drains to the Sound.

That means all of us—the 4.5 million people who live, work and play in the Puget Sound basin and who also affect water quality.

Our challenge is getting larger. Tony Wright, the executive director of the Puget Sound Partnership, notes that by 2040, the population in the Puget Sound basin will swell to seven million, which is equivalent to adding a city the size of Portland, Ore., to the region.

Each year, hundreds of tons of toxic organic chemicals and metals find their way to the Sound from cars, roofs, wood burning, boat paint, household pesticide use, consumer products, fertilizers and other sources.

For many people, it was easier when we could blame big industry for our pollution woes. Now, when we look for the answer, we only have to look in the mirror.

In recent years, much of Puget Sound cleanup planning has been completed. Now we are in an even more difficult phase. To get things done, people will have to change their lives, and, in many cases, it won't be easy or cheap. Replacing a leaking septic tank can cost $10,000 or more. Dairies and hobby farmers may have to keep bacteria in animal waste from entering streams and rivers.

Asking people to change their practices and spend money to help clean up the environment will not be easy. At a meeting to discuss efforts to reduce fecal coliform discharges into the Samish, Department of Ecology Director Ted Sturdevant told me, "We are getting a lot of resistance to our effort to go door to door to get folks, primarily the livestock owners, to adopt different practices."

The push-back resulted in bills by legislators to restrict Ecology's ability to impose penalties.

When I became governor, I knew the effort to clean up Puget Sound would not be easy. As state Ecology director and later as attorney general, I watched two separate agencies, the Puget Sound Water Quality Authority and the Puget Sound Action Team, struggle with cleaning up our troubled waters.

Frustrated with our efforts, I scheduled lunch with Congressman Norm Dicks, a long-time champion of restoring Puget Sound. We met in a small café, and the more we talked about the need for action, the more animated our conversation became. Staff members later told us that other customers in the restaurant stopped talking to each other and focused instead on our lively Puget Sound discussion in the corner.

As a result of my discussion with Norm, I convened a panel of Washingtonians in 2005 to study clean-up efforts across the country and make recommendations for preserving the health and ecosystem of Puget Sound. I also wanted to help educate and enlist the public in achieving recovery of the Sound by 2020. I called the panel the Puget Sound Partnership—partnership was the key word. Past efforts resulted in "random acts of restoration."

I knew it would be critical to select just the right person to chair the panel, so I turned to Bill Ruckelshaus, a statesman and corporate mover-and-shaker with an impressive environmental track record.

Bill rose to the public limelight in 1973 when he resigned as deputy U.S. Attorney General rather than follow President Nixon's order to fire Watergate Special Prosecutor Archibald Cox.

He was the first head of the Environmental Protection Agency and later returned for a second stint. Bill then served as a corporate executive before returning to the Northwest to work on a variety of successful environmental initiatives.

I liked Bill's philosophy and track record in getting local groups to work together. We had tried to clean up the Sound from the top down with a heavy-handed, regulator approach. Now we needed a partnership approach, and Bill was the guy to do it.

Bill teamed up with Jay Manning, then the director of the Department of Ecology, as a co-chair, to lead the panel, which included Norm Dicks, Northwest Indian Fisheries Commission Chairman Billy Frank, Jr., King County Executive Ron Sims, UW President Mark Emmert and a list of other notable Puget Sound leaders.

By the end of 2006, the panel had delivered its recommendations. With these in hand, I proposed legislation in 2007 to establish the Puget Sound Partnership as a new state agency.

I turned again to Bill Ruckelshaus to lead the Leadership Council of the new agency. And I chose David Dicks, a passionate, articulate advocate for Puget Sound, as the agency director. When Bill retired in 2010, I appointed Martha Kongsgaard to replace him.

The Partnership wasn't created to be a regulatory or cleanup agency. It wouldn't issue penalties for toxic discharges. It wouldn't regulate industry. Instead, its job was to coordinate and lead more than 700 federal, state, tribal and local agencies in 12 counties and 110 cities working to clean up the Sound.

The legislation also directed the Partnership to develop a science-based plan so clear, measureable goals could be created.

The GAO study recommended many of the changes we had written into the Partnership bill, such as involving the public and developing a single recovery plan with measurable results that has broad support. As one news reporter wrote, the Partnership "was created to be part planner, part persuader, part banker and part cheerleader."

Five years after the Partnership was created, the record on cleaning up the Sound is mixed.

The Partnership's 2012 "State of the Sound" report shows that we have slowed the decline, but progress has not been sufficient to meet 2020 recovery targets. We are still losing ground in some areas. For example, the total number of Chinook salmon in Puget Sound has declined.

At the same time, there are successes: better water quality; restored salmon habitat; nearly 1,400 acres of shellfish beds reopened for harvest; and about 2,300 acres of completed habitat restoration projects.

There also has been innovation. The Navy is working on a new idea for mitigating the environmental impacts of underwater construction for its new wharf in Hood Canal. Instead of trying to mitigate development projects one by one, site by site, the Navy proposed starting an "in lieu fee" program, allowing mitigation to be done at the local level.

Anyone who needs to build a dock, and it involves environmental impacts, could pay into a new fund as a condition of getting a permit. Combined with funding from the Navy, the program would invest in the highest-priority salmon restoration projects for Hood Canal. I joined the celebration of this new watershed mitigation program when it was approved in 2012. The program offers great potential to clean up the whole Hood Canal watershed, save the salmon for future generations and do both more efficiently and effectively to the benefit of all parties.

Another early success was the decision in 2012 by the Department of Health to upgrade 750 acres of shellfish beds in Oakland Bay near Shelton. This area is home to 19 commercial shellfish companies that provide 274 jobs and produce manila clams, oysters and mussels with a market value of more than $9 million. The original shellfish industry was wiped out by pollution in the 1920s.

The success was a classic example of what needs to be done when there is no single polluter. Public improvements were made to Shelton's wastewater treatment plan. Homeowners invested in improvements to on-site septic systems. Farm practices were upgraded.

By the end of 2012, the Department of Health will open another 280 acres of commercial shellfish beds in Hood Canal, the direct result of providing sewer capacity in the Belfair area to replace failing septic systems that drained to the Canal.

Dewey believes that, overall, we are making progress. "The wins are hard, and sustainable wins are even harder," he said.

The public, meanwhile, is impatient for more results like the Oakland Bay and Hood Canal successes. People want to know the beaches in their favorite bay have been reopened for fishing, swimming and shellfish collection.

We need to show people we are getting things done on the ground and that we really are making progress. It's all about results.

We also have encountered new challenges—such as ocean acidification. Global emissions of carbon dioxide have increased the acidity of the ocean waters, in turn affecting the ability of oysters, clams and other shellfish to reproduce and grow.

Scientists are warning things will get worse before they get better, and when I visited the Taylor Shellfish hatchery in 2010, I was struck by the implications to Washington state. The industry exports high-quality shellfish to countries around the globe and supports hundreds of jobs. It depends on clean water.

Washington is particularly vulnerable to ocean acidification. The storms in the Pacific cause what scientists call upwelling, where water from deep offshore is brought to the surface along our coast. This deep water is more acidic since it carries carbon dioxide emissions, which were absorbed by water on the surface decades ago. Over time, as the water settled to the bottom, it mixed with organic matter, which further increases the water's acidity. These acidic waters are then pushed to the surface in the turbulence from the storms off our coast.

Though Washington is only one small state, I couldn't let this go without trying to make a difference, at least for future generations. In 2011, Dr. Jane Lubchenco, the National Oceanic and Atmospheric Administration administrator, and I agreed to launch the Washington Shellfish Initiative, the first regional program under a new federal program to support commercial and recreational shellfish.

As part of the Initiative, we decided to convene a blue ribbon panel on ocean acidification. We put the scientists, policy makers and opinion leaders all in the same room, and charged them to make progress together.

The panel produced a comprehensive review of the science and a road map for how we can proceed. Included in the report were ideas about how we can help the shellfish industry adapt to the changing ocean, where we can take local action to reduce ocean acidification, and where we can lead by example in reducing our carbon dioxide emissions.

The response to the panel's recommendations, and to our commitment to take action, was amazing—with news reports filed around the world.

It reminded me why states need to lead, rather than wait for others to act.

The GAO study said it is still unproven whether you can clean up an estuary the size of Puget Sound with millions of people living along its shores. I am not ready to give up. We face a long-term incremental shift that requires individuals to change their behavior. It won't be easy but the stakes are too high not to try. I am betting that over time, the farmer or septic owner up stream will ultimately do what it takes so the farmer downstream on a Puget Sound bay can enjoy a clean watershed.

The Radioactive Reservation

IN THE LATE 1980's, while serving as director for the state Department of Ecology, I flew into the Tri-Cities Airport in Pasco and was met by a highly unusual greeting party.

A small group of workers from the Hanford Nuclear Reservation were waiting to protest my efforts to force a more aggressive cleanup of the 586-square-mile site, which is one of the most contaminated places on earth.

Each worker carried a broom, and they complained that my cleanup demands would turn them into janitors. One worker shouted that I could take his broom and use it to fly home.

Ever since 1942, when the Manhattan Project chose Hanford as the site to produce plutonium for the bombs which would help end World War II, Hanford employees have been accustomed to working in a shroud of secrecy and have had no intrusion from outsiders, like state officials.

That all began to change when the U.S. Department of Energy, which runs the Hanford site, was forced in 1985 to release more than 19,000 pages of documents, which confirmed the extent of contamination.

U.S. weapons production at nine Hanford nuclear reactors produced 43 million cubic yards of radioactive waste and more than 130 million cubic yards of contaminated soil and debris. In addition, about 475 billion gallons of contaminated water was discharged to the soil, resulting in more than 80 square miles of groundwater contamination.

The mix of radioactive and chemically hazardous wastes was an environmental nightmare and would ultimately become the world's largest environmental cleanup.

There was one other big problem with the Hanford contamination—the Columbia River flowed right through the middle of the site and there were plumes of radioactive groundwater slowly flowing to the river. As a result, the state had a huge interest in the quality and speed of cleanup. But the federal government and its contract employees, as evidenced by the broom brigade at the airport, didn't want us involved.

That was the scenario I inherited when I took over as head of Ecology. For more than two years I skirmished with the Environmental Protection Agency and Energy over cleanup plans. I realized a lawsuit was always an option, but I was convinced going to court was not the answer. Given the size and complexity of the cleanup, I believed we all had to be in the effort together. Litigation should be the last tool in the tool chest.

Instead of a long, contentious lawsuit, we finally agreed in 1989 to manage the work under what was called the Hanford Federal Facility Agreement and Consent Order, or, as it is more popularly known, the Tri-Party Agreement.

I negotiated the agreement with Mike Lawrence, Department of Energy Hanford manager. It was a highly antagonistic relationship at the start, but as we worked together we became friends, and Mike even gave me a broom, with a Tri-Party Agreement logo on it, to commemorate our work.

The agreement was just the start of our work, however. I learned that it is an unending battle to make sure the federal government funds the cleanup, makes good decisions, and makes continued progress.

The cleanup, which costs about $2 billion annually, is slowly progressing. At one time, there were hundreds of plumes of contaminated groundwater heading for the Columbia. Today, thanks to federal stimulus money and the world's largest pump-and-treat system, only one plume remains.

The next big challenge is stabilizing 56 million gallons of highly radioactive and chemical waste in 177 massive underground tanks—66 of which are known leakers.

The plan is to build a vitrification plant that will blend the waste into glass-forming materials. Once in glass form, the radioactive wastes will be more stable and safer to store. They will, however, have to remain in storage for thousands of years as the radioactivity safely dissipates.

That's the plan, but getting the facility built remains a huge challenge. It will be the world's largest plant of its kind and will be one of the most complicated facilities ever built on the planet. Completion of the plant continues to fall behind, partly for funding reasons, partly due to management issues, and partly due to technical challenges.

In the past, construction has proceeded in fits and starts. When a technical issue arises, construction is stopped and another study is conducted. We have delayed too long. While we have to take every concern seriously, Energy should expedite the process by having the nation's technical experts on hand to address issues in real time without stopping construction.

It also is challenging to get cleanup funding annually from Congress. Hanford and the Tri-Cities community were there for the nation when plutonium for warheads was produced at the site. Now it is time for the nation to be there for the community and fully fund the urgently needed cleanup.

With the stakes so high, the state needs to stay on top of the work to make sure the federal government stays in compliance with the cleanup agreements. The days of the broom brigade are long gone, but federal officials and their contractors nevertheless need a governor looking over their shoulder to ensure restoration of Hanford is a statewide priority.

A Name You Will Never Forget

PROTECTING OUR MOST VULNERABLE CITIZENS

THE DAY AFTER I was inaugurated on Jan. 12, 2005, Tyler DeLeon, a seven-year-old kindergartner, who was dehydrated, had multiple abrasions on his right leg and shoulder, and who weighed just 33 pounds, died in a Spokane hospital.

The excitement from the previous night's formal inaugural ball quickly gave way to the harsh, heartbreaking responsibilities of holding the office of governor.

The state's Child Protective Services (CPS) office had received a number of reports of injuries to Tyler, with the last coming from school officials who reported Jan. 4 that bruises covered his face.

But no one investigated, and nine days later, little Tyler died.

"The case raises serious questions about the role of the state's child welfare system," an article in the *Spokesman-Review* newspaper in Spokane noted.

State government is responsible for protecting our most vulnerable citizens, including our children, the elderly and the developmentally disabled. It is hard to fathom the abuse Tyler and others endure. Equally disturbing is the extent of abuse. In 2011, CPS conducted almost 38,000 investigations for abuse or neglect.

At the other end of the age spectrum, Adult Protective Services conducted more than 13,000 investigations.

That means on any given day, there is an average of 140 complaints about a child or senior enduring some form of abuse or neglect. Each day, bad people are doing bad things to other people, and while it may be impossible to stop all tragedies like the one that occurred to Tyler, we need to do everything we can to prevent them.

Managing programs to protect our vulnerable citizens is a tough, complicated, gritty job. As governor, I realized it is important to come back to the basics, to pound in that safety is the number one priority and to continually fight complacency. The Tyler case and a lack of sufficient oversight of adult family homes serve as cases in point.

The Spokane newspaper was right—more should have been done to protect Tyler from his adoptive mother, Carole Ann DeLeon.

That's why, when I interviewed Robin Arnold-Williams to be my new director of the Department of Social and Health Services (DSHS), a key topic was response times to cases of child abuse and neglect. Robin, then the head of Utah's Department of Human Services, was surprised to hear that up to 10 days were allowed in Washington to respond to allegations, well beyond the national norm.

The tragic implications of a slow response were driven home when I slid the Tyler DeLeon case file across the table to her.

Robin was a 25-year veteran of human services, so she knew how tough a job state workers have to protect society's most vulnerable citizens. "You never forget a child's name after a case like this," she said.

DSHS includes Child Protective Services, which is responsible for protecting children from abuse or neglect. I don't know what we would do without people who are willing to work as CPS caseworkers. They see things done to innocent, helpless, trusting children that are unimaginable.

CPS caseworkers, at any given time, are working on an average of more than 23 cases. They spend their days looking into the darkest, most horrific side of human behavior. Yet they come back day after day, determined to make life better for a child.

In addition to those caseloads, they face intense pressure. If a caseworker removes a child from a home, the family is angry, and so too are parents' rights groups. And if the child is left in the home and something happens, children's advocates and others demand the caseworker be held accountable along with the division chief, the DSHS secretary and the governor.

"You just have to know when you take these jobs horrible things are going to happen, even if you do things right," Robin will tell you.

But everything wasn't done right in Tyler's case. After I hired Robin, her job and mine was to find out what more could be done. We owed it to Tyler to stop abuse and neglect from happening to another child or adult.

We knew we needed to respond faster to reports of abuse and neglect. But the question was how to do it. There was no money for more caseworkers. Our decision was to change the culture in CPS.

When we came into office, we found that Children's Administration, the DSHS division where Child Protective Services is housed, had said yes to too many demands for additional work from legislators, advocacy groups and the federal government. Each demand, of course, did not include money to carry it out.

Robin and I knew we had to take some of the pressure off and send staff a clear message: They were expected to prioritize child safety. We told caseworkers we know there is pressure to do other work, and we know that work may not get done, but they are to never doubt, never forget, that safety of children is the number one priority.

We set a 24-hour response time target for all cases with an emergency child abuse report and 72 hours for non-emergencies. We also told the caseworkers we would work to get more staff and reduce caseloads.

The old adage is that what gets measured gets done, so we included 24-hour response as one of the goals I would be tracking for DSHS in my Government Accountability and Measurement Program (GMAP). That meant Robin would have to appear every few months before me and my senior staff in a televised public forum and report whether the agency was meeting the response times and other goals.

The GMAP forum demonstrated to staff my commitment to goals and that the 24/72-hour response was prominent on my agenda. Sure enough, the agency responded. When we started measuring responses within 24 hours, we were meeting the goal 60 percent of the time. Today, initial emergency responses occur within 24 hours more than 99 percent of the time and non-emergent responses occur within 72 hours close to 98 percent of the time.

Robin and I also knew rapid response alone wasn't the answer. We needed to make sure staff was doing high-quality investigations, so we also tracked occurrence of repeat abuse in GMAP. We found that repeat maltreatment dropped from a little more than 12 percent of the cases to about 6 percent.

As an assistant attorney general and later as attorney general, I was aware of the tough job CPS staff have, so after we met our goals for faster response times, I sat down and personally signed 400 letters thanking individual caseworkers for their efforts.

Senior citizens are another vulnerable population, and protecting them would also require a culture change in DSHS.

For years, many of our old and frail residents were cared for by family members. Then private residences—called adult family homes—opened up. They were cheaper to operate than nursing homes and offered a friendlier, non-institutional setting, often in neighborhoods and close to family and friends. In many cases, family members cared for an aging parent, grandparent or aunt or uncle, so these adult family homes were regarded more as "mom and pop" facilities.

With the growth in our elderly population and the need for long-term care, there was a growing reliance on adult family homes. Soon they had transitioned from "mom and pop" homes into a rapidly growing industry that now included profiteers and individuals ill-equipped to care for the elderly.

DSHS focused its human and financial resources on the nursing-home industry to meet federal standards. Oversight of adult family homes failed to keep pace with the rapid growth and changed culture in what had become an industry, not just a trend.

It was a classic case of an agency getting too comfortable and complacent and not recognizing changes in the volume and quality of care in for-profit adult family homes. Low entry fees and the promise of profits—homes could charge up to $5,000 a month—resulted in a flood of new homes. At one time, there was a new home opening every day.

Most people failed to recognize that unlike nursing homes, where there was a strong regulatory structure in place and plenty of people around to report abuse and neglect, adult family homes were flying under the radar with cheap licensing fees, little scrutiny and few inspections.

That was the view until the explosive *Seattle Times* series "Seniors for Sale" painted a disturbing picture of life in some homes. Reporter Michael Berens found that about 11,200 seniors were living in more than 2,800 adult family homes, many of whom were exploited or harmed by their caregivers.

Berens wrote that, "The *Times* uncovered accounts of elderly victims who were imprisoned in their rooms, roped into their beds at night, strapped to chairs during the day so they wouldn't wander off, drugged into submission or left without proper medical treatment for weeks."

This important series clearly indicated major shortcomings in our regulatory system. It never helps to make excuses, and the allegations were serious; I recognized we needed both immediate actions as well as a review to identify additional steps to protect our elderly citizens.

I called for a complete review within the next two days and ordered that DSHS require homes to post investigative reports so families would be aware of problems. I also ordered DSHS investigators to immediately start making more thorough investigations of complaints and post investigative results on its website.

In the end, our review produced more than a dozen recommendations for new laws and procedures to improve oversight of the industry. It was time the state stopped subsidizing for-profit adult family homes. Licensing fees were increased to allow us to hire more enforcement staff. Training for staff was required, and fines were increased to put more teeth in enforcement.

Our changes have helped, yet the Legislature balked at imposing higher license fees to pay for staff, so we still lack the ability to fully inspect and investigate adult family homes. While we have made great strides in oversight, we could do better.

DSHS faced different demands in its Division of Developmental Disabilities.

For years the department operated five residential habilitation centers (RHCs), which are facilities for individuals with disabilities.

The RHCs had strong support from family members and guardians who felt their loved ones were safest and received the best care in the centers rather than in community residential settings.

In recent years, however, home and community-based services have emerged as the favored option for most advocate groups. They believe people with developmental disabilities do best when they live, play, work and receive services in a community setting. The community option is also less expensive than RHCs.

MaryAnne Lindeblad, who was a DSHS assistant secretary until I named her to head the state's Health Care Authority, said for years the department heard competing demands from institutional and community-based advocacy groups.

I had personal interest in this issue. My cousin, Ronnie, was developmentally disabled and thrived in the community—so much so that he lived more than 30 years longer than doctors expected. He was loved by everyone in his neighborhood who came in contact with him.

Prior to taking office, there had been an attempt to close an RHC in King County. But there was so much resistance that the closure plans were beaten back and I didn't revisit the idea during my first term.

The Great Recession, however, forced us to reexamine everything the state was doing, including the operation of RHCs. Every other state was moving away from institutionalization—10 states had already closed all their institutions.

The policy challenge for DSHS was to strike a balance between two emotionally charged views. Even though many groups felt community settings offered a better life experience and were less expensive, the department wanted to respect individual and family needs and choices for their loved ones.

In the end, under the leadership of then DSHS Secretary Susan Dreyfus, we succeeded in closing one institution, the Francis Haddon Morgan Center in Kitsap County. We also imposed a restriction on new admissions to institutions of youth younger than 16.

Key to the success of our proposals was the work by DSHS to increase services and support available in the community.

Families received information and support in moving loved ones to community residential settings. The new Parent Mentor program helps families identify services and options that best meet their needs. The Roads to Community Living program offered the services of a three-member transition team to help families cover all aspects of the move, including medications, meal planning and employment.

To assure a successful transition, DSHS also set up quality assurance teams to assess each individual's move to the community residential setting.

Another key component was the decision by DSHS leaders to emphasize employment of youth and adults with developmental disabilities. As a result, the state has become a national leader with its level of employment rising from 53 percent in 2004 to 89 percent in 2011.

The key to success was recognizing the value of work and the need for collaboration between the private and public sectors. As Robin explained, "We have the expectation that everyone should have the right to work."

Another challenge for DSHS staff is they often find themselves caught in the middle of difficult public policy debates over protecting public safety versus civil rights. The disturbing case of Isaac Zamora is a classic example.

On Sept. 2, 2008, Zamora, who lived near the tiny Skagit County town of Alger, went on a shooting rampage and killed six people, including Deputy Sheriff Anne Jackson. Zamora later told investigators, "I kill for God."

Zamora entered guilty pleas to 18 charges, including aggravated murder, attempted murder and burglary. He pleaded not guilty by reason of insanity to two other aggravated murder counts.

Despite the guilty pleas, the not-guilty-by-reason-of-insanity pleas meant Zamora was not sent to prison, but instead to the forensic unit at Western State Hospital, which is one of the two psychiatric hospitals for adults operated by DSHS. Laws aimed at preventing the criminalization of the mentally ill provide for individuals found not guilty by reason of insanity be remanded to the state hospital for treatment.

At the same time, to remain certified, hospitals like Western State have to provide safe treatment environments for the mentally ill. So, on the one hand, DSHS is trying to offer a suitable facility for treating the mentally ill, while on the other, they are trying to protect the residents, staff and society from extremely dangerous people.

It has cost DSHS more than $1 million a year to have additional staffing and two Department of Corrections officers guard Zamora 24/7.

In December 2012, DSHS transferred Zamora from Western State to a secure facility operated by the Department of Corrections. The transfer occurred under a 2010 law that allows the transfer if the patient, who has been found not guilty by reason of insanity, is an unreasonable safety risk in the hospital setting.

This is not an isolated case. There are other dangerous patients at state hospitals and they pose huge challenges for balancing mental health treatment and safety. In too many cases today, in Washington and around the nation, we have a situation where a hospital, focused on treatment, is increasingly being asked to ensure safety when treating individuals who have committed horrific acts of violence.

Protecting and helping Washington's most vulnerable citizens is a tough but incredibly rewarding job. Staff faces a relentless flow of complaints and demands for services, yet despite the workload, as we learned with young Tyler, the stakes are high with no margin for error.

As governor, I learned it helps to always return to the basics. Focus first and foremost on safety. Fight complacency. Have respect for your clients and do all you can to provide them with the rights, responsibilities and opportunities for a full, rewarding life.

Indian Country

IF YOU WANT A QUICK LESSON on the role of history and culture in governing, just take a look at the state of Washington's $87 million misadventure with construction of a dry dock in Port Angeles.

About a month before I took office, I learned the state was walking away from the project, which was intended to produce much-needed replacement pontoons for the east half of the Hood Canal Bridge. The bridge was reaching the end of its structural life.

Initially, the state Department of Transportation (DOT) project progressed smoothly. Work had begun on a graving dock, which was a term, we would soon learn, that was incredibly unfortunate. The graving dock was a pit, adjacent to the shoreline, where the pontoons would be built and then could be floated away when the site was flooded.

An initial investigation of the site found nothing of historical or archaeological value. But during excavation, crews made an alarming discovery. They unearthed a pre-European settlement village which was at least 2,000 years old and is called Tse-whit-zen by the Lower Elwha Klallam Tribe.

Equally alarming was the discovery of more than 335 intact skeletons. Here is how *Seattle Times* reporter Lynda Mapes described the scene: "It was midmorning on Sept. 21, 2003, when excavators doing a second archaeological survey dug up a human skull, its eye sockets staring up from the backfill of an old utility trench."

DOT had invested in what was an ancestral and spiritual home for the tribe. "As you know, from the beginning this has been a difficult, and even painful, subject for our tribe. We have already suffered damage to ancestral remains and losses of historic properties, and it has become clear that—no matter how hard we all worked at it—the current construction cannot be sustained," Lower Elwha Klallam Tribe Chairwoman Frances Charles wrote to DOT.

As a result, on Dec. 21, 2005, the state walked away from the Port Angeles project and later shifted pontoon construction to a site in Tacoma.

The Port Angeles debacle is a reminder that in this fast-paced, high-tech era, where people are always looking ahead to the next big "thing," we have an obligation to take the time and make an effort to protect our rich culture and history.

Knowing Washington has tens of thousands of archaeological and cultural sites and an unknown number of burial sites, I knew after taking office we had to do something to try to stop new missteps in the future.

To do that, I issued an executive order directing all state agencies to work with the Department of Archaeology and Historic Preservation and the tribes to more thoroughly review capital construction projects and land acquisitions to determine any cultural impacts.

I wanted agencies to thoroughly examine the project area to see if cultural resources were present, and to work more closely with tribes, which have a deep knowledge and reverence for archeological, historical, religious and ceremonial places from the past.

Communication and consultation with the tribes has to occur in far more areas than cultural resources. Washington has 29 federally recognized tribes and that means each is a sovereign government with treaty rights.

Relations between the tribes and state government have never been easy, and can be downright rocky on some issues. The law on tribal issues is incredibly complex, misinformation abounds and cultural differences can create serious misunderstandings.

Like most things, having close, personal contact with elected leaders of tribal governments helps maintain strong state-tribal working relationships. I have been fortunate to have a good relationship with many tribal leaders over the years. We do not always agree, not by a long shot, but I have always appreciated the can-do attitude they bring to problem solving and their willingness to continue to engage on difficult problems.

I recall one challenging meeting with Chairman Brian Cladoosby, from the Swinomish Indian Tribal Community, and Chairman Ron Allen, from the Jamestown S'Klallam Tribe.

While both have become close friends of mine over the years, we certainly have had our disagreements. At the end of one of our more "robust" discussions, I turned to the two of them and said, "What happened here? Did you decide to play bad cop and worse cop on me?" In typical good humor, Chairman Allen said, "I was supposed to be the good cop, but I forgot, and once I got going, I just couldn't stop."

Washington state's tribal populations have been in this area for thousands of years. Their treaties with the United States pre-date the admission of Washington into the Union by more than three decades.

As a lawyer who understands that treaties are the supreme law of the land according to our federal constitution, I appreciate the many nuances in the relationship between the state of Washington and our tribal governments. As the governor of the state, I accepted the gentle chiding by the tribal governments that I led the "baby" government.

When dealing with Northwest Indians, you learn that teasing is part of the culture and a sign of respect.

Washington state has had its share of challenges with its tribal governments, from armed conflict in the 19th century to fish wars in the 20th century. Former Governor Booth Gardner and a group of tribal leaders met and decided we had spent enough time fighting and should work together toward common goals. The Centennial Accord agreement, which called for, among other things, annual meetings between the state and tribal governments, was the landmark result of those discussions. It was signed in 1989, 100 years after Washington's statehood.

I was Gardner's Department of Ecology director at the time. I helped write the Accord and believe I have attended every Centennial meeting since.

While we've had our ups and downs, like every relationship, the Accord has become a forum through which we can deal with everything from law enforcement to transportation, health and social services, to natural resources and economic development. The meetings have ranged from incredibly productive to frustratingly painstaking. Still, year after year, now through four governors and dozens of tribal leaders, we continue to come together to look for solutions to vexing problems.

The meetings have generated good will and understanding and helped forge strong working relationships. As a result, we have been able to negotiate agreements about how to share tax proceeds from cigarette, fuel and liquor sales. We've worked on challenging law enforcement and child welfare protection agreements. We've agreed on common interests related to salmon recovery and the cleanup of Puget Sound. We agreed to jointly pursue legislation allowing high school credit for the study of tribal languages and we built curriculum for the study of tribal history and culture.

The Accord process supported the inclusion of Indian Law on the Washington State Bar exam for incoming lawyers, and it produced legislation allowing tribal governments to purchase insurance coverage for their employees through the state's insurance program. The list is long and varied. Through it all, we've called each other to action and held each other accountable.

For me, the Accord reminds us to respect the sovereign status of the tribes and be willing to consult and communicate with them.

If we do that, we can solve problems and keep incidents like the graving-dock debacle from happening again.

Demons of War

OUR DEPARTMENT of Veterans Affairs (WDVA) received a letter one day about its post-traumatic stress disorder (PTSD) program. To me, the letter summed up the great challenges and opportunities we have in serving those who served.

"Without this program I am not sure I would be alive today," the veteran wrote. "I'm an older vet; I suffered from drug addiction, alcoholism, and was alone except for family and work. I beat the addictions, but family and work left me, and the depression and nightmares stepped in to reclaim this time."

He added, "Without your help I would be without help or hope. I understand what the demons of war have done, and what I can't change I can try to understand and deal with in positive ways (most times), and when I can't, I have help. Thank you WDVA, a grateful vet."

He also complained about the availability of service from the federal Veterans Administration and said with WDVA that, "I can reach out in time of crisis and share with other vets who know or have been where I am at."

The letter reminds me about the terrible things war can do to our servicemen and women, and if we want to serve them well when they return home, we have to focus completely on delivering services that are convenient, peer driven and address multiple needs.

Washington has one of the fastest growing veteran populations in the nation and has nearly 670,000 vets. The number will grow since the nation has been through its longest period of war in its history with Operation Iraqi Freedom and Operation Enduring Freedom in Afghanistan. More than 10,000 members of our National Guard alone have been deployed in those theaters.

Not since World War II have we seen such a large-scale call-up of our National Guard and reserve units.

It is estimated that about one-third of the men and women returning from war will have invisible wounds like PTSD.

I must admit, I have a personal interest in veteran's issues because my husband, Mike, is a Vietnam vet. We saw how this nation treated our returning Vietnam veterans in the late 1960s and early 70s. There was little appreciation and respect for their service, and programs to help them readjust were inadequate and largely inaccessible.

No wonder the greatest percentage of our homeless vets are from the Vietnam War era.

It also is no wonder that Mike chose helping vets as his top priority as the state's "First Gentleman."

It also is personal to me because I went to Iraq to meet with members of the Washington Guard who were deployed there. I had no entourage—just me. I couldn't tell anyone but Mike and Adjutant General Tim Lowenberg that I was going. For security reasons, there was virtually no notice.

Even after that trip, I can't pretend to understand what all our troops went through in Iraq. I do know, though, that wearing a helmet and flak jacket was incredibly hot and uncomfortable in the desert sun. Sand blew everywhere and settled in your hair and mouth. Most troops were living in cargo containers that had no air conditioning, not even in the mess hall.

These young men and women left families behind, endured unbelievably tough living conditions and put themselves in harm's way, all because their nation called. I couldn't have been more impressed or humbled.

It is not that I hadn't listened and understood what Mike was saying before. But that experience made me an even bigger believer in the huge commitment we must keep with our troops. And that is why I support WDVA's goal of establishing Washington as the most veteran-friendly state in the nation. To help accomplish that, we worked successfully on 91 bills aimed at helping our veterans and military personnel.

I have learned there are a number of challenges in effectively serving vets. Two big ones stand out to me. First is getting their attention when they come home from war. When 22-year-old soldiers return home, they have a lot more on their minds than a briefing on veteran benefits. If the choice is between seeing a loved one or hearing a briefing on the GI Bill, I know what the likely choice will be.

The other problem has to do with the nature of veterans. They aren't inclined to come home and ask for help. Often, they don't think they need help, and they don't know the rules or have the time to figure them out.

Another reality is that many veterans don't realize they are entitled to benefits, so we made a special effort to educate them about the help available. This not only helped prevent future problems, it also meant we were able to get federal dollars to the vets and this reduced the burden on our state budget.

While it may be hard to get the attention of returning vets, it is absolutely vital to identify problems as early as possible because you can prevent negative things from happening in the future. Getting help for PTSD today may help head off substance abuse, joblessness, domestic violence or other issues tomorrow.

With our history of Vietnam vets in mind, WDVA Director John Lee, who also is a Vietnam vet, and Mike were committed to "get it right" this time when our warriors returned home.

To better serve returning troops, in partnership with the state Military Department, WDVA redesigned demobilization procedures. In the past, troops had to sit through a three-hour slide presentation. Now the department brings in teams of specialists to meet the returning troops and they hold one-on-one meetings. Pre-printed forms allow staff to enroll soldiers in programs they are qualified for right on the spot. This hands-on, person-to-person approach has resulted in a much greater percentage of vets getting programs they are entitled to.

The other big change is to provide what WDVA calls a spider web of touch points. John knows many veterans don't live near big cities where most services are located, and they won't travel 200 miles to get them. So he contracted with veterans service organizations to bring the services to the vets. It costs about $1.6 million for the current two-year period, but the outreach has resulted in 17,000 claims that average about $500 in federal benefits. That amounts to $8.5 million in payments, but, more importantly, it helps prevent more serious problems in the lives of the veterans.

The agency has also decentralized PTSD counseling so service can be delivered in the communities where vets live. About 1,800 veterans a year use the service. Lee has found vets are reluctant to seek counseling from someone without PTSD experience, so the counselors are skilled at war trauma.

While the Great Recession has been hard on employees across the nation, it has been especially difficult for soldiers returning from combat. For many, the Army has been their only job, and, frankly, the lower-ranking enlisted troops return to a tight job market without a lot of civilian job skills.

When in Iraq, each unit I visited asked questions about sports teams, and other home-state topics, but the most common query was, "Will I have a shot at a decent job when I get home?"

Sadly, some return home with marketable job skills, but war injuries prevent them from picking up their career in the civilian world. Still others had skills and experience that weren't easily transferrable to stateside jobs.

Lee and his team knew the key was to get to the veterans early. The first step was working with the state Employment Security Department to get vets unemployment benefits to carry them through until they could land a job.

Teams also went through the unemployment rolls to find veterans, and then connected them with their WDVA benefits, including education and training in high-demand fields. Partnerships with businesses and apprenticeship programs also helped open doors. In addition, I directed state agencies to reach out to veterans.

We also realized we could help returning vets by helping their spouses.

Many had business licenses in other states before moving to Washington with their husband or wife. So I successfully requested legislation that required licensing agencies to expedite the right of qualified military spouses who were transferred here to receive a Washington license. Sometimes just cutting through the red tape made a big difference.

Other bills required licensing agencies to evaluate military training and experience for credit toward meeting state licensing requirements.

Mike, John and veterans organizations discovered a big hole in our service network for families. For years, the only veteran's cemetery and veteran's homes were located in Western Washington. It seemed disrespectful to make a surviving spouse or children of a fallen warrior drive 10 hours roundtrip to visit the grave of their loved one.

Lee found that the state could get a federal grant to build a cemetery, but the state would have to cover operating costs. With a deep recession and massive state budget cuts facing us, we knew it would be highly unlikely to get $350,000 in annual maintenance costs through the Legislature.

So veterans' organizations went to work and gathered more than 12,000 signatures for armed forces license plates to fund the cemetery maintenance.

The plates went on sale in 2006, and, in 2010, several thousand people joined Mike and I on a cold, wet and windy day to witness the dedication of the cemetery in Medical Lake. It was the culmination of a dream for many families east of the Cascades.

As the ceremony ended with a flyover from Fairchild Air Force Base and a lot of teary eyes, the crowd realized veterans who had sacrificed so much now had a final resting place closer to family and friends.

Funding to construct a veteran's home was even more challenging to secure, but the design is finished. We have set aside $14.4 million in state funds and have applied for a federal match of $21.7 million. John hopes to have a facility open in 2014.

WDVA also has moved to what it calls wrap-around services. A program called Building 9 for Veterans Transitional Housing has 60 beds for those in need of stable housing, vocational rehabilitation and sustained income. Staff is on hand to provide the range of services needed to help the vets return to the community, including chemical dependency programs, mental health services and employment assistance.

As soon as I took office, Mike told me he felt the need to go to as many funerals for fallen service members as possible. He wanted to be there for the families to thank them personally and show respect for their fallen warrior on behalf of the state. Little did we know what his commitment would mean. During my term, I wrote more than 340 condolence letters to families of servicemen or women lost in the line of duty. Watching families who have lost a mom or dad, a son or daughter or a niece or nephew reminds you what war really means.

It also reminds us that we owe it to those who return from war to do all we can to deliver the services that can help them escape, as that one veteran said, "the demons of war."

Call Out the Guard

I AM SURE Washingtonians would heartily agree that during my two terms it seemed I had to deal with more natural disasters than in any other eight-year period in memory.

It looked as if I was not only constantly signing disaster declarations, it also seemed like I was signing many more than my predecessors.

Turns out, that's right. I signed 32 disaster declarations during my administration, averaging about one every three months, compared to just 16 by my predecessor, Gov. Gary Locke.

Wind, snow and rainstorms. Wildfires, mudslides and landslides. Droughts and floods. It seemed we were constantly pounded by a disaster that threatened the lives and livelihoods of Washington residents.

Most people think of storms when it comes to disasters. In September 2012, however, there were no storms. In fact, Washington was enjoying a spectacular string of beautiful, sunny days. Then, on the evening of Sept. 8, dry lightning lit up the Central Washington sky and touched off 75 fires in tinder-dry forests.

For the next three weeks, fire crews struggled to contain massive fires started that night. Two of the fires, the Wenatchee Complex Fire and Table Mountain Fire, would burn more than 80,000 acres and thousands of firefighters would be required to bring them under control. Smoke from the fires blanketed Eastern Washington and created hazardous air quality in Wenatchee and other areas.

When you run for office, you don't usually think about this part of the job. But I learned there are few things you do that are as important as responding to disasters that leave people in emotional, physical and financial distress. With that in mind, my first cabinet appointment was to make Major General Timothy J. Lowenberg head of the National Guard and the state's Emergency Management Department.

Governors, and all state elected officials for that matter, should be well versed in emergency-response procedures, and make sure they can respond quickly and effectively when disasters strike.

Even when disasters occur as often as they did on my watch, the relentless pressure of other business makes it easy to let down your guard when the Emergency Operations Center closes and people slowly begin to piece their lives back together. But that is exactly the time state government needs to conduct after-action reviews to identify lessons learned, so you can run exercises and better prepare for the next disaster.

No matter how much you prepare and how often you drill, every disaster brings something new or different, so you must be able to quickly handle the routine in order to focus on the unusual.

In the United States, disaster response is primarily the responsibility of state and local officials who best know the people and the communities. One of the most critical resources a governor has is the state National Guard, which she or he commands.

It is important to fight to retain control of the Guard. I know, because we almost lost that control to the federal government.

To help you understand this issue, let me give you a couple examples.

In December 2007, a horrendous wind and rainstorm pounded the Washington coast and inland areas such as Lewis County. The storm unleashed flooding that hit areas in the upper reaches of the Chehalis River particularly hard.

Pastures were flooded. Trucks and cars were nearly buried in mud. Houses and barns were isolated in mudflows up to 6 feet high. Interstate 5 in Chehalis was below 7 feet of water and closed for days.

"All you can see are the peaks of roofs—it is difficult to comprehend," I told the media after flying over the disaster zone.

The storm struck rapidly. One woman told a *Seattle Times* reporter she was taking a shower when she noticed water bubbling up from the drain. When she looked outside, she found the house surrounded by water, and by the time rescuers arrived by boat, water was gushing into the upper level of her home.

Hundreds of people found themselves in similar situations and had to be rescued by crews in boats and helicopters. The airlifts and boat rescues were carried out by the National Guard, Coast Guard, local emergency-response crews and other organizations.

That is the way things are supposed to work: a coordinated response, under clear command, with good communications.

Compare that with Hurricane Katrina. When news reached us about the havoc caused by Katrina, I immediately called Louisiana Governor Kathleen Blanco and asked if we could help. "Send your National Guard," she replied.

I called up our Guard and its members were among the first to arrive in the storm-ravaged Gulf region. They were put in charge of running air operations throughout the rescue and recovery operations. The work of Washington and other state Guard units was remarkable. By some accounts, the Guard saved 17,000 people and relocated 70,000 more.

Despite a lot of good work, after-action reports revealed serious response problems. The federal and state response was found to be slow, disjointed and inefficient. One of the most egregious problems was the lack of integration between the National Guard and active-duty federal forces sent to assist.

Remember, you want to execute the routine response flawlessly, so you can focus on the unforeseen.

Unfortunately, instead of producing thoughtful ideas about how to coordinate forces in the future, the Katrina after-action reports prompted years of bickering before a solution was identified to help government better respond during the next disaster.

The Department of Defense (DOD) had language put into the 2007 National Defense Authorization Act (NDAA) to give the president the authority to take control of the National Guard in domestic emergencies. Despite a loud, unified protest by governors, the act was ultimately passed with language that would have allowed a president to call up the Guard in specific instances: to aid in natural disasters, terrorist attacks and other cases.

The provision would have overturned the 200-year-old Insurrection Act that prohibited the president from activating the Guard except in rare circumstances, such as putting down a rebellion.

After an intense lobbying effort by governors and other groups, Congress relented and reversed this change in the 2008 NDAA. But the change left unresolved the question of how, in future disasters, the Guard and federal troops would better work together. It was the intent of Congress in the NDAA that the then-Bush administration would bring together governors and federal officials to identify the best course of action(s) to resolve this "unity of effort." President Bush, however, did not do so during the remainder of his second term.

The governors offered ideas to solve the problem, but they were rejected by DOD, which was still supporting presidential call-up of the Guard. Many Guard officials complained about "arrogance" within DOD, where staff viewed the Guard as "weekend warriors" and felt governors were not able to respond to disasters.

"The governors and the Guard are on the ground in our communities, and know the people. They are best prepared to respond in an emergency," said Mark Rupp, my Washington, D.C., representative who worked this issue. In military jargon this is called "situational awareness."

The National Guard is the face of security, he added. "When people are in trouble, they say 'call out the Guard' not 'call out the army.'"

In January 2010, President Barack Obama did what Congress was looking for in the 2008 NDAA and established—by executive order—the bipartisan Council of Governors. He appointed me co-chair along with Vermont's Republican Governor Jim Douglas.

The initial talks were agonizingly slow and contentious. I believe some Pentagon officials came to the table feeling burned over the fact that governors had succeeded in reversing their legislation. Frankly, nobody was banking on our success.

Mark is less charitable. After sitting through hours of meetings with DOD officials arguing over every word and phrase, he calls the Pentagon "the land of 10,000 lawyers."

Ultimately we were fortunate that key players helped break the bureaucratic inertia: Defense Secretary Robert Gates and Homeland Security Secretary Janet Napolitano.

Gates was a problem solver. As my colleague Gov. Douglas paraphrased Gates' message: "Let's cut to the chase. You don't want to give up your prerogatives as commanders in chief of your National Guard. We don't want to give up the president's constitutional authority over the armed forces. So we have to find a way to work this out."

Napolitano was the former attorney general and governor of Arizona, and had on-the-ground experience commanding the Guard and working on disasters.

Also helpful was Federal Emergency Management Agency (FEMA) Administrator Craig Fugate, who ran Florida's emergency management agency for eight years before heading up FEMA.

Ultimately, DOD agreed unity of effort was essential and that paved the way for Congress to approve legislation and provide for a trained and certified National Guard officer, or, in some rare cases, a commissioned federal military officer, to be put in charge of all troops responding to a disaster as a "dual status commander." The appointment requires presidential authorization and approval by the affected governor.

Since passage of the law, Washington has trained and certified several Guard officers who are now ready to lead a joint state-federal effort. Most states do, as well. In fact, in the devastation brought on by Hurricane Sandy along the East Coast in October 2012, the governors of New Jersey, New Hampshire, Massachusetts, New York, Maryland and Rhode Island all appointed dual-status commanders to lead the National Guard and federal forces.

In Washington, the Emergency Management Division is located in the

Military Department, which is also home to the Guard. This is so the adjutant general can work on a seamless plan to respond to emergencies. With the new law, federal troops can also be added to the response effort.

During the 32 disaster declarations I issued, the Guard was called up 11 times. Hopefully Washington won't have a need to bring in federal forces for a long, long time, but if we do, we have procedures in place to do it right.

Calls in the Middle of the Night

DEALING WITH TRAGEDIES

ON A QUIET SUNDAY MORNING in November 2009, I was enjoying time with Mike at the Executive Mansion.

As Governor, your life is scheduled in 15-minute increments, and you are sent home each night with a foot-high stack of reading materials and paperwork. So I was appreciating the chance to relax and talk with Mike.

When the phone rang and Washington State Patrol Chief John Batiste came on the line, I knew immediately something terrible had happened.

A lone gunman had burst into a coffee shop near McChord Air Force Base (now Joint Base Lewis-McChord) and opened fire on four Lakewood police officers who were working on their laptops, catching up on paperwork at the beginning of their morning shift.

The ambushed officers, Sergeant Mark Renninger, 39, Officer Tina Griswold, 40, Officer Ronald Owens, 37, and Officer Greg Richards, 42, all died in the attack.

Following one of the largest manhunts in the region's history, the gunman, Maurice Clemmons, was shot and killed by a Seattle police officer two days later.

Nothing prepares you for the terrible tragedies that occur on your watch as governor. You can try to prepare yourself for the unexpected, but there is always something new, tragic and untimely.

While you have a lot of power, the first twenty seconds of that call from the Chief reminded me how helpless governors can be, and, as much as you wish it were so, you just can't reach out and bring those officers back to their families and loved ones.

You find you have brief periods when things are going well, only to have those moments shattered by tragedies like the killing of the Lakewood officers.

A little more than two years later, I received another weekend call. This one came late Saturday night, and I knew it couldn't be good news. I was right. This time it was Eldon Vail, my Department of Corrections secretary.

Eldon reported that 34-year-old Corrections Officer Jayme Biendl had been found dead in the chapel at the Monroe Correctional Complex. Jayme had ended her shift at 10 p.m. but had not reported back from the chapel or turned in her equipment. She was later found strangled with a microphone cord.

The suspect in the killing, Byron Scherf, 52, confessed to killing Jayme. Scherf is already a three-strikes offender serving life in prison for rape convictions.

Once again, it was a call that makes you want to cry. Tragedies like those that occurred in Lakewood and at Monroe call on governors to act with their hearts and their heads.

While it is impossible for a governor to ease the pain for families, you can be a great source of compassion and support for family and friends and let them know how much the service of their loved ones meant to the rest of us, and that they died making life safer for others. They served no higher calling.

The other obligation we have is to use our power as governor to do our absolute best to prevent similar incidents. While we will never be able to stop bad people from doing bad things, we can learn from tragedies and look for safeguards that will help others.

By most estimates, the memorial service and procession for the Lakewood officers were the largest in state history—more than 2,000 cars were in the procession.

Lakewood Police Chief Brett Farrar initially planned to invite only people who personally knew the officers to speak at the service, but he later invited me. In this highly politicized world, he was worried that a governor might leave an unfavorable impression.

The chief's concerns are not without precedent. A remarkable woman named Gayle Frink-Schultz saw it happen. Gayle is head of an organization called Beyond the Badge; they help critically injured law enforcement officers, maintain the beautiful Law Enforcement Memorial on the state Capitol campus, and help families of fallen officers.

As part of her work, Gayle helps with memorial services for officers killed in the line of duty. She witnessed a time when an elected official approached the memorial with an attitude of "what they could gain and not what they could give from the heart."

Governors attend memorial services not for themselves, but on behalf of all the people of the state, and must send the clear message that we all are indebted to those who gave their lives for us.

I was pleased to learn later, after the initial cloud of grief had receded, that Chief Farrar was glad he invited me. He said I was able to bring some kindness and compassion to the service. "The service was about the people who lost their lives and those left behind trying to pull their lives back together," he said. "I think the families were overwhelmed by the amount of love and support they received."

At memorial services, you watch as families try to hold it all together, but each time I brought the state flag to them, they just broke down.

"Long after the memorial service is over, that flag, or the photo of a governor at the service, is a memory families can hold onto," Gayle explains. "It says the governor of the state took the time to be there for them. It is hard at the moment but huge in the long run."

She knows. On March 22, 1993, her husband, 39-year-old Washington State Patrol Trooper Steven Frink, died from injuries he received when he was thrown from his motorcycle on an Interstate 90 off-ramp when a car he was pursuing spun out of control.

I also learned that expressing emotion isn't a weakness. I remember choking up at the memorial for Seattle police officer Timothy Brenton who was killed in a drive-by shooting in November 2009.

After the service, I told John Lane, one of my policy advisors, that I was frustrated for losing it. He told me not to worry about it, because when he talked to law enforcement officers after the ceremony, they said that moment told them that I was feeling the same pain they were.

The second role of the governor requires more management skill and more head than heart.

Clemmons, the killer of the Lakewood officers, was out of prison despite a teenage crime spree in Arkansas. His 108-year prison sentence was commuted by then-Governor Mike Huckabee. Officials in both Washington and Arkansas were criticized for letting Clemmons be free.

Following the death of the Lakewood officers, I knew well-meaning legislators would be lining up to sponsor bills to address issues in the Clemmons case. But sometimes in the haste to correct a terrible wrong, rapidly written legislation can be ineffective or have unintended consequences.

To make sure we had a calm, thoughtful, deliberative process, I organized a work group that included all the organizations that represented law enforcement, prosecutors and judges. The group was able to pull together a package of bills that, ultimately, moved easily through the Legislature.

Governors are ultimately accountable for anything that happens in state government, so I felt I needed to play an active role in addressing the Monroe tragedy in which Officer Biendl was slain. I believed we would need a thorough, transparent investigation, and that we needed to candidly acknowledge any findings and then use them to make all changes necessary to improve the safety of our corrections officers.

I also needed to make sure leadership at Corrections was very clear about these goals, and that while I didn't plan to manage the investigation, I would be checking back regularly and holding the department accountable for results.

To make sure we got an impartial review, we called in the National Institute of Corrections (NIC), which provides technical and programmatic reviews and critical incident investigations. I also attended the first meeting of the NIC review committee to make sure its members understood I wanted a thorough review and that I expected them to receive complete access to get the information they needed.

About two months later, when the review was complete, I made another decision. If the public was going to believe in this investigation, I decided I needed to announce the findings and not delegate it to Corrections officials. And we decided not to announce it from Olympia, but rather in Monroe, the hometown of Jayme's family, friends and colleagues.

A key finding by NIC investigators was a sense of complacency among staff. People were just too used to routines, and that meant they were not ready for the unexpected. It is a lesson that every organization needs to constantly remember—especially in state government, where so many of our agencies are responsible for public safety.

In my announcement, I said Corrections needs to improve alarm systems, add staff and reduce overcrowding. I also vowed to ensure changes were made. "Jayme's legacy will be enhanced protection of her coworkers who face inherent dangers while on the job," I said.

To do that, I developed executive request legislation, which passed the Legislature and implemented some of the NIC findings. In addition, Corrections was directed to follow through on other recommendations from the report and staff. As a result, more than 1,500 security concerns were investigated and processed.

We all learn lessons that later help us solve problems or manage our organizations. But the tragedies that occur under any governor's watch never get easier to handle emotionally and are never the same.

Given that America was entangled in two wars during both my terms, news of the death of a Washington soldier or the loss of a law enforcement officer became too common. I wrote more than 340 condolence letters to families of servicemen or women and 26 letters to families of law enforcement officers, all lost in the line of duty.

People often ask what the most difficult part of the job is. To me, it is attending services for fallen law enforcement officers or members of the military. The grief you feel for the family, friends and colleagues left behind is overwhelming. But as difficult as funerals and memorial services can be, it is helpful to remember, as Gayle Frink-Schultz explained, we can provide great comfort and support for families and friends who have endured a horrible loss.

Changing a Culture

A FALL MORNING in 2009 turned out to be a very, very uncomfortable time for staff from the state Department of Community, Trade and Economic Development (CTED).

The CTED folks were gathered before me at a public session of my Government Management and Accountability Program (GMAP). In addition to a roomful of observers, the session was broadcast by TVW, which is the equivalent of C-Span except it covers state government.

Among the topics on tap that morning was CTED's program to weatherize homes for low-income families. Washington received $59 million in economic recovery funds for weatherization with a target of 7,000 homes by June 30, 2011.

The data that morning showed the agency was unable to meet its production goals, completing just 68 of the planned 500 units. The delays in weatherizing homes not only put future federal funding at risk, but also took away an opportunity for low-income families to save 20 to 30 percent on their cooling and heating bills.

That morning session was obviously very frustrating to me. I couldn't understand why the agency wasn't alarmed by its performance and why it hadn't already taken steps to improve the timeliness of installations.

While frustrated, I also wasn't completely surprised. Beginning back in my days as Attorney General, I was concerned about the ability of state government to measure the results of its programs and hold staff and managers accountable for results.

There was simply no culture of performance management across state government.

I also knew that even when agencies recognized problems, there was a long, hard road to fixing them. As I said in speeches to agency managers, when government identifies a problem, there is a tendency to form a committee where staff talks about the problem and then talks about it some more. Next there are emails, lots of emails. Then comes the research, and later, a little more research. Ultimately, memos are dispatched around the agency about possible next steps which may, or may not, fix the original problem.

Based on this history, I was convinced I had to do something about changing the management culture when I became governor in 2005. To do that, I started two initiatives—GMAP (Government Accountability and Performance) and Lean.

I had first experimented with GMAP as Attorney General. The idea is based on a system called CompStat which is an accountability program successfully used by the New York City Police Department under Police Commissioner William Bratton. The program was credited with bringing down the crime rate in the city by 60 percent.

The idea behind GMAP is that every agency, every program, and every employee must be accountable for results that matter to citizens. It is all about making sure taxpayers get value for every tax dollar. State agencies need to use data to provide real-time information to determine whether programs are working, and if not, they need to be problem solvers and change them or eliminate them.

That is exactly what happened in the case of weatherization. Just a few months later, staff had turned the program around to the point that I announced, "You got your people going, and as a result, the U.S. Department of Energy assistant secretary called me and made it clear how pleased they were at the dramatic turnaround, and it was so dramatic that they put us on a short list of states to get additional funds."

In the end, CTED weatherized 9,000 homes—2,000 more homes than their original target. We saved more than 200,000 BTUs for low-income households, and we put hundreds of people back to work.

State agencies have several levels of GMAP measures—statewide and internal. Every quarter, agency directors have to report GMAP results to me and my management team. The forums are public sessions and are televised by TVW.

Our goal is full transparency at the forums. We air the good news and the bad. At times, I have been asked by directors not to discuss certain topics at the forums because the results are not good. My answer to them was always the same—to get full accountability, we need to admit when we are not performing well.

When we aren't achieving the results we want, the purpose of the forums isn't to make the agency directors squirm. It is all about getting us back on track so we get results. We have a conversation about why we aren't hitting our targets. We talk about what strategies the agency has to improve results. And since I have my management team on hand, we talk about what we can do to help.

The tough GMAP sessions end with a plan to do things differently. We establish clear goals, assign responsibility to lead the new effort, and set timelines.

As uncomfortable as the forums can be, I was surprised to hear that a survey of agency directors found they believe they are important, both for accountability and problem solving, but also for public education.

When we started GMAP there was a lot of grumbling in the agencies about it being the management trend du jour. Some staff groused that we have a new governor with a new management idea; we will just have to outlast her.

For that reason, I was pleased to learn in my last year in office that agencies, when asked how important GMAP is, gave it an aggregate rating of 4.95 on a scale of one to five, with five being "very important."

While GMAP focuses on data to measure performance, Lean was started to improve government processes, again to ensure citizens get value out of every tax dollar. It provides principles, methods and tools to develop a culture in state government that encourages employee creativity and problem-solving skills to improve value and service. Lean is a well-known management tool and technique in the private sector, but had never been adopted into the culture of state government.

Because the private sector was so experienced at Lean, and because our budgets were so tight during the recession, I asked various business-es to help and they responded in a big way. Boeing, Impact Washington, Virginia Mason Medical Center, Group Health Cooperative, Alaska Airlines, Starbucks, Seattle Children's Hospital and Premera all provided support for our Lean transformation efforts.

Like GMAP, it takes time to incorporate Lean into the culture of state government. We called it our Lean journey. A little more than a year and a half after we started an enterprise-wide Lean effort, more than 6,400 em-ployees and 1,600 leaders had been trained in Lean thinking, tools and techniques and every executive cabinet agency had started work on Lean and completed at least one Lean project.

More importantly, Lean projects are getting results by reducing agency workload backlogs, improving the quality and consistency of inspections, speeding up permit approvals, and allowing more staff time for "mission critical" work, which improves morale.

I have to admit I may not have recognized it at the time, but the methods I used to roll out GMAP and Lean were different, and, fortunately, best fit the needs and situation at the time.

GMAP was rolled out in a more formal and direct way. As a new gov-ernor, I knew GMAP worked and I didn't think I had the time to slowly roll it out across state government. I wanted to quickly establish a culture based on results and performance management, so I hired Larisa Benson, a bright, young Evans School of Public Administration grad with experi-ence in performance measurement, to start a mandatory GMAP program for the agencies.

For Lean, I knew from the private sector that it works, but I believed we needed to find out how it would best work in state government. I decided to have Larisa's successor, Wendy Korthius-Smith, lead a slower rollout so agencies could explore Lean options, approaches and philosophies and learn how Lean would best work for them. We also had the advantage of the generous support from the private sector, which allowed agencies to begin using Lean with the help of experts guiding the way.

We essentially had the "willing and able" begin using Lean in their agencies. Importantly, their work allowed us to record some real successes, and employees began to rave about how it empowered them and helped them redesign their work. Word spread and soon the fence-sitters began to get more interested.

At that point, I decided to direct that agencies begin making Lean a part of their culture and issued an Executive Order for a Lean transformation.

Lean is not about saving money, it is about reducing waste, improving quality and service, and increasing productivity. During the recession, state staffing was dramatically reduced while the demand for services and number of people served increased. So in addition to better serving the public, Lean was intended to help staff survive at a time of diminished resources and higher demand.

For years, state government measured performance on the number of permits it wrote, inspections conducted, people served or licenses issued. But no one asked what we were really getting for all those permits, licenses and inspections. GMAP has put us on a track to help tell people exactly what they are getting and Lean is helping us get to those results in a more efficient, productive and effective way.

A Sea of Red Ink

BUDGETING DURING AN ECONOMIC CRISIS

As I rose to give my State of the State address to a joint session of the Legislature on Jan. 15, 2008, I was feeling pretty good about the news I was about to deliver.

After all, the number of jobs in our state had risen by 218,000 over the past three years and our unemployment rate was the lowest in our history.

A larger education budget allowed us to cut class sizes, boost salaries to teachers and staff, add early learning slots and increase admissions at our community and technical colleges as well as our four-year universities.

Exports from our heavily trade-dependent state were up 50 percent, and *Forbes* magazine had listed Washington as one of the five best states to do business.

We had provided health insurance to 84,000 more kids and were on the way to having every child covered in the near future.

My budget had a $1.2 billion surplus and my proposal for a rainy-day fund, to help the state through tough financial times, had been approved by voters the previous fall.

True, the state revenue forecast from the previous November predicted that state revenue would be down by $132 million over the next two years. Yet Dr. Chang Mook Sohn, executive director of the state's Economic and Revenue Forecast Council, said the decline was due to an earlier-than-expected repercussion from a slowdown in real estate activity. He added that the housing and construction sectors in Washington were still outperforming the rest of the nation.

Just days later, the World Bank predicted a credit crunch would slow the world economy, and, on Jan. 21, global stock markets suffered the steepest drop since 2001.

There are clear signs, Sohn responded, that the U.S. economy is slowing down.

"Slowing down" became an understatement. Few people realized at the time that we were headed for the deepest and longest recession since the Great Depression, with terrible consequences for families, businesses, state government and the nation.

The November forecast of a $132 million revenue shortfall would be just the first round of dismal news. Over a catastrophic period of a little more than four years, 17 of the 19 quarterly revenue forecasts were negative.

Washington would endure record-unemployment levels, unprecedented numbers of mortgage foreclosures and huge, new demand for state services. Families were thrown into unemployment and clamored for health care, help paying utility bills, food assistance, hospice care for aging parents, and more.

People who had never needed help in their lives suddenly found themselves out of work and facing foreclosure on their homes and desperate for assistance. One day, while I was handing out items at a food bank, a man came through the line and said to me, "I have been here many times, but, until today, I was always on your side of the table."

Any recession imposes hardships on people. What made this recession so pernicious was its duration and depth. During past recessions, state government would make a round of difficult cuts and wait for the rebound. At times, it felt like this Great Recession would never hit bottom.

Over the next four years, state government would be forced to make budget cuts again, and again, and again. It took six special legislative sessions over a four-year period slashing state budgets to stay in balance. For perspective, in my first four years there was just one special session and it lasted one day.

By the time we had a positive forecast, we had cut state spending by more than $11 billion and laid off 7,500 workers, taking the state workforce to levels not seen since the mid-1990s.

The relentless cutting consumed the time of managers who had to figure out how to make the reductions. It sapped employee morale, and, of course, had devastating impacts on millions of people across Washington.

Unfortunately, when state revenues decline, the demand for services increases. The Great Recession was no exception. While state revenue fell 7 percent, the number of people requesting Temporary Assistance for Needy Families jumped nearly 30 percent; the number seeking medical assistance jumped 22 percent; and the number of people in state-supported nursing homes or community-care settings jumped 12 percent.

As the recession's havoc grew, I searched for guidance in our state's history and from states around the nation, but I found little help. In fact, most states were asking *us* for guidance. I realized we were on our own, and we learned some hard lessons about budgeting in dire times over the next four years.

Drastically cutting budgets just once is a difficult task. This Great Recession, however, offered its own special pain. It was relentless. Just as we completed one difficult round of cuts, a new forecast would come out and we would have to find ways to make more cuts to a budget we already thought was bare bones. It was an emotional grinder. Every cut had human impact: reducing service to people with developmental disabilities; slimming down child-care services; cutting assistance to out-of-work single moms; or telling merchants there is less money to treat mentally ill street people who scare off customers.

I had exceptional budget directors, Victor Moore, Marty Brown, and, for the last part of my term, Stan Marshburn. Their budget staffs were professional, bright, knowledgeable, caring and creative.

But beyond them, it is lonely, hard work.

I often felt like I was alone on the floor of an arena with one arm tied behind my back, being circled by lawyers who were threatening lawsuits, and scanning the stands filled by special-interest lobbyists all yelling that I should preserve their programs.

The fact is a governor has limited discretion in making budget cuts. There is an old adage that the state's job is to educate, medicate and incarcerate. That reflects the fact that about 60 percent of state spending is for basic education, federally mandated Medicaid programs, prisons and other programs, and, for the most part, all are off limits for cuts.

Lawsuits pose another huge limitation. The state was sued more than a dozen times by groups opposed to our cuts. In 2011, for instance, a Thurston County judge rejected the state's effort to save more than $30 million by restricting non-emergency visits to hospital emergency rooms.

It was frustrating to have people come in and make a budget pitch only to find they insisted on looking at the budget in silos. The education people would say cut social services, and social-service people would say cut education. And, during those first rounds of cuts, all I got from people is, "don't cut us."

In the next rounds, I started to tell them, "I can't hear you unless you say where I can cut." I learned that nearly everyone who came to me were advocates (paid or not) and that they will not advocate against their self interests.

A state budget is a policy statement, and every budget ultimately comes down to real people. My lengthy budget meetings with staff started with numbers, but it didn't take long to get down to people.

I remember the day we had a budget meeting on a Saturday morning before I attended a memorial service in Aberdeen for a woman who was like a second mother to me. She had been scheduled to use hospice care to help make her final days more comfortable and easier.

Sure enough, on the agenda that morning was a proposal to make massive cuts to the hospice budget. To this day, I don't think my budget staff knows why I had to hurry from the room to compose myself.

Over the four-year period, I met with budget staff for hundreds of hours, and much of the time was spent making heart-wrenching decisions. It was common for us to take brief breaks while a staff person wiped away a tear after a particularly tough discussion. I realized that, while I ultimately had to make the decisions, it wasn't easy on budget staff who were working long, hard hours and felt saddened by the work they had to do.

The human impacts of cuts aren't always obvious. For instance, podiatry services are considered optional under Medicaid. We had a proposal to eliminate the program. I asked staff, "As a recipient of these services, who am I and what would happen to me if I had no podiatry services?" "You could lose your foot," Carole Holland, my senior budget analyst for human services bluntly replied.

From then on, to help me better understand the impact of budget cuts, I'd ask staff, "Who am I and what does this mean to me?" That way the cuts weren't just numbers—they represented real people with real consequences.

I also learned it is important to make sure people understand they aren't the only ones taking deep cuts. That's one of the reasons I held a Saturday budget session in November for my cabinet directors, along with my budget and policy staff. We reviewed an early draft of my proposed budget, divided into subject areas.

Hearing all the cuts I was proposing allowed directors from each agency to hear what other agencies were going to suffer through. It wasn't just one agency affected by the cuts. All felt the pain. Directors from natural resource agencies could hear what I was proposing in education and human services and general government. They all could understand the hard decisions and trade-offs I was considering. Directors left with a deeper understanding of the very difficult choices we had to make as a state and a renewed respect for each other's work.

Because of the impact cuts have on people, I learned that making budget decisions in a deep recession is tough politically and personally. There is a small segment of the population whose very existence depends on state aid. Many are mentally ill; some have drug or alcohol addictions; still others are totally incapable of holding down a job and have virtually nothing. As the cuts continued to go deeper and the realization of the effects on these people spread, the number of death threats against me increased. I remember realizing I was cutting, suspending or eliminating programs I had supported and worked for my entire life.

I went through what was like the five steps of grieving, and when I came out the other end, I was clear on what I had to do: steer state government through the recession and do all we can to position the state so it could emerge ready to succeed in a rebounding economy.

Someone once said a crisis is too important to waste, and I adopted that theme. "We must not only cut, we must restructure, modernize, reprioritize and position our state for the 21st century," I explained. "It's not just about this crisis—it's about setting our state on a trajectory that ensures a strong financial foundation for our kids and grandkids."

The recession allowed us to make reforms that would have been politically impossible in normal times. We consolidated agencies, closed state facilities, eliminated boards and commissions, and reformed our unemployment insurance, state employee pensions and workers' compensation systems (see chapter on government reform).

Some said that despite the fact I had pushed through a rainy-day fund and supported large budget surpluses, I should have saved more. Yet no one—including our chief economist—predicted the depth and length of this recession, and no one would have predicted we would end up cutting more than $11 billion.

I remember one gentleman respectfully telling me I was to blame for the economic crisis. I asked if I was responsible for the crisis just in our state or the other states, too. He said, "fair enough, I'm just frustrated."

As the recession wore on and we made succeeding rounds of cuts, I felt it was important to get more people involved to not only generate new ideas, but also to inform the public about the budget challenges. As I traveled around the state, I found a considerable number of people who believed there was fat to be eliminated. Or, as my budget staff said, people really believed the budget could be balanced by cutting the Department of Fraud, Waste and Abuse.

If there wasn't fat, others insisted there was an untapped pot of gold. They didn't want services to be cut, but they also weren't willing to pay more taxes. I'd remind people that more than six million Washington residents don't use our prisons, but they all still want safe communities. More than five million people don't depend on state-funded mental-health services, but they didn't want a mentally ill individual menacing their family as they walked down the street.

One editorial page opposed new taxes and cuts in education, particularly higher education. In 2011, facing a cut of $2 billion on top of the $8 billion in reductions made in previous years, we challenged that newspaper to draft a budget. They quit after identifying $250 million in cuts, at which point Marty Brown reminded them they still had $1.75 billion to go.

There is nothing like a budget crisis to bring out quick-fix ideas. By making one little change it would seem you can avoid tough cuts to schools, colleges and social programs. While easy fixes relieve the pain today, they create agony in the future. In 1971, for instance, legislators added a 25th month to the state's 24-month budget cycle. It gave them an extra month of revenue collections, but it left the next budget cycle short one month. It took 16 years to buy back the pay day-type loan.

In the summer of 2010, I launched the "Transforming Washington's Budget" process. As we began reviewing agency budget proposals, we asked tough questions, including:

- Is the activity an essential service?

- Does state government have to perform the service or can it be provided by others?

- Can the service be eliminated or delayed in recessionary times?

- Does the activity have to be paid for with state General Fund dollars?

The Transforming Washington's Budget Committee comprised 36 business, nonprofit and governmental leaders. The committee conducted four town hall meetings around the state that drew more than 2,000 people. We used ideas gathered in these forums to make budget decisions.

We also developed an interactive website that offered the public a chance to contribute and participate. The site drew 19,000 visitors who offered 137,000 votes on budget-cutting ideas submitted by site visitors.

In addition to standard budget-cutting actions, like reducing spending on travel, equipment, consultants and new hires, I challenged agencies to find innovative ways to do business. One successful idea came from the Department of Revenue, which, with legislative approval, enacted a first-ever tax amnesty program.

Under the program, the state would waive penalties and interest for a qualifying business that paid agreed-upon late taxes, allowing businesses to resolve old tax issues. During the three-month amnesty window, nearly 8,900 businesses paid $343 million in back taxes.

As I end my term, I realize the state budget is the one blunt instrument the state uses to respond to the recession. There were no easy fixes. There were no easy choices. All you can do is make the best choices you can and take a long view that will help prepare the state to come out of the recession stronger than when it started.

As governor, you come into office with an agenda. You are always advised to stick to the agenda—don't let others, natural disasters, or anything else keep you from accomplishing what you set out to do.

All that is fine, but if you are hit with a major economic crisis, you have to pivot and embrace only one agenda: use your head and heart to steer the state through it so we come out stronger, better prepared and with the values of our state intact.

The Time is Ripe for Reform

USING A CRISIS TO REFORM STATE GOVERNMENT

TOP MANAGERS of the state Department of Licensing gathered in Director Liz Luce's office on a gray January day in 2009, not knowing about the surprise that awaited them.

They had come to her office to watch my second inaugural speech before a joint session of the House and Senate. The team knew the economy would be a big part of the speech given the deepening recession, skyrocketing unemployment and growing state revenue shortfall, all of which were forcing massive state budget cuts.

The previous year, I asked agencies for ideas that would result in "21st century government reform." Among the ideas was a proposal to close licensing offices. "It was a rudimentary idea that we really hadn't developed," recalls Alan Haight, who was on Liz's executive team and later took over as director when she retired.

As the team watched, they heard me say, "We can close 26 licensing offices across the state while extending hours of operation at the 10 most popular locations."

"A growing sense of dread came over the room," Alan recalls. "We didn't really think we would be asked to close offices due to the highly charged, political nature of the decision."

In a normal year, Alan's point would have been absolutely right. The Legislature had no appetite for this kind of reform before the recession, and, after steep cuts in 2009, they believed and argued that we didn't need change because we would emerge from the downturn and get back to normal just like in the past.

When the economy didn't bounce back, I began to sense the time may finally have come for reform. Legislators had grown weary of taking big cuts to their favorite programs, and I believed they would finally consider government reform in exchange for smaller cuts to the budget.

I knew that even with a massive economic crisis, reforming government wouldn't be easy. In state government, you have to be careful when you create a new board, commission or office because, once created, it is extremely difficult to get rid of it.

Peek into every corner of government and you will find an agency or program with legislative patronage. Some are huge, like the Department of Social and Health Services (DSHS) with 15,600 employees. Some are tiny, like the one-person Citizens' Commission on Salaries for Elected Officials. While agencies differ in size, they all have one thing in common—a vocal constituency with a fierce sense of survival.

That is how it is with government reform. There may be a program or policy 80 percent of us would cut or eliminate, but there is another 20 percent that feel absolutely passionate about it and, when people are passionate, there is usually a legislator willing to fight for their cause. As with any legislation, it is much easier to kill it than pass it.

Everyone knows that the big, expensive issues in Olympia, like workers' compensation, water rights, public safety and health care, are so highly charged politically that it is nearly impossible to have a civil, let alone reasoned, discussion about changes or reductions.

Yet, ironically, with all the resistance to real reform, everyone in Olympia demands reform. When you ask them what they have in mind, however, it invariably is some highly partisan idea that, if enacted, won't save money or improve service to the public.

As I geared up for reform, I realized we needed to come up with real reform that not only saved money, but also put the state in a stronger position to emerge from the recession with a sustainable budget.

I developed three reform goals:

- Eliminate state offices, programs, boards and commissions that had outlived their usefulness, could be carried out in other ways, or weren't essential from a cost-and-service standpoint;

- Bend the cost-curve to make programs less expensive, more efficient and more sustainable; and

- Streamline service delivery.

It is hard to believe, but I learned the last time a state facility was closed was 14 years ago. That gives you an idea of how hard it is to close a state facility. I knew, therefore, we had an uphill fight, even to close a Licensing office.

There are legitimate economic, service and other issues that have to be considered before closing offices. Especially for Licensing. "As an agency vilified by the public for long lines, delays and confusing procedures, we knew closing offices would be unpopular," Alan explained.

Licensing tackled the problem by expanding self-service and online options so fewer people would need to go to the offices. The goal was to reduce wait times for people who wanted face-to-face interactions. Over a three-year period, the agency increased self-service transactions by 500 percent and moved about 700,000 transactions out of their offices.

Legislators told licensing staff they supported closing offices—so long as it wasn't one in their district. The agency, however, was ready for that argument because they had been strategic in targeting which offices to close. They looked at travel distances for customers, the cost-per-transaction for each office, office size, lease arrangements, and the capacity for remaining offices to absorb new business.

Alan said they also were strategic in selecting the first office to close. It was in Auburn, my hometown, and just a few miles from another office in Kent. "We figured if we can't close Auburn, we wouldn't be able to close any office," Alan said.

The Auburn office was later closed, despite the best efforts of my driver education teacher from high school, who reminded staff he taught me how to drive and was going to personally call me about the closure.

In the end, Licensing closed 11 offices and reduced the hours or days of operation at another 14.

One other barrier to institutional closures is that they often are key economic engines, particularly in rural communities. Usually, they are the largest employer in town and inject significant funds into the local economy. I'm sure there still are negative feelings in the small town of Naselle, located in southwest Washington, where we tried to close a youth camp.

Ultimately, the recession and the need to modernize government overcame local resistance and we closed a number of institutions, including Maple Lane School, a juvenile rehabilitation facility, and three prisons—Ahtanum View, Pine Lodge and McNeil Island. We also closed Frances Haddon Morgan Center and moved its residents, people with developmental disabilities, to community settings.

My second goal was to reduce the cost of state government, not only for today, but well into the future so we could have a more sustainable budget.

The biggest fight was over reform to the state's workers' compensation system. The program, which is run by the Department of Labor and Industries (L&I), pays medical expenses for workers who suffer work-related injuries or illnesses and partially replaces lost wages if they are unable to work due to those conditions. In some cases, injured workers are entitled to permanent-disability awards and vocational assistance.

Workers' compensation has always been a hot-button issue between labor and business. Labor fights to protect injured workers and business fights to keep premiums down.

During my first years in office, there was little or no growth in premiums. In fact, in 2006 and 2007, L&I returned more than $350 million to employers and workers in the form of a "rate holiday."

Then the Great Recession hit. Investment earnings for the fund decreased, and premium payments declined as more people lost their jobs. At the same time, time-loss claims and pension payouts were increasing.

With premiums shrinking and liabilities growing, L&I had to draw down its reserves. Judy and I knew we had a problem since it is hard to keep rates low when you are burning through your reserves. But how do you raise premiums when businesses are failing or struggling to survive in a recession?

Especially alarming was the dramatic increase in the number of injured workers receiving lifetime pensions. In the mid-90s, one in 45 time-loss claims was a pension. By 2010, it was one in 20. In just 12 years, pension payments grew from $250 million to $700 million—8 percent of the claims were driving 85 percent of the costs.

Judy Schurke, my L&I director, shared my concern that the cost of the program simply was not sustainable.

We also worried about the loss of skills and productivity in our workforce as more injured workers took pensions instead of finding new opportunities to work.

In 2011, I announced a reform package as governor-request legislation. My decision immediately touched off a pitched battle between business and labor.

I convened a bi-partisan group of legislators to try and find a compromise, and immediately ran into problems. For most, the battle lines were drawn. Business lobbyists hovered outside the doors to our meetings. Labor refused to participate. Some at the table were new to this complex issue and were (legitimately) worried about making decisions that were potentially worth billions of dollars and had major impacts on people's lives.

I called in the business lobbyists and told them they were going to blow any kind of agreement if they continued overreaching. Next, I made it clear to labor that the status quo threatened the entire system. But, most importantly, I brought in experts who could explain details of workers' compensation. I asked tough questions that represented the concerns of stakeholders and people at the table. Slowly, we moved out of the realm of politics and into a thoughtful discussion about policy.

In the end, however, it was politics that finally carried the day. I often heard about the division between Republicans and Democrats. Actually, during my terms as governor, it was more a division between the House and Senate. In this instance, the Senate said it would block passage of a budget unless action was taken on some key reform bills, including workers' compensation. Ultimately, meeting in my office, the House and Senate finally reached a compromise and agreed on the biggest reform in 40 years. The bill saved an estimated $1.5 billion over the next four years.

We also got bipartisan support for reforms to the other state program that pits labor against business—the state's unemployment insurance program.

During the recession, unemployment insurance trust funds went bankrupt in 36 states and were forced to borrow from the federal government. But, because we have maintained one of the healthiest systems, I was able to convince the Legislature in 2011 to pass reforms that provided businesses with $300 million in tax relief and extended benefits to nearly 70,000 families across the state.

Our state's pension plans have long been among the best funded in the nation. But despite the solid funding, they, like individual investors, took huge hits in the recession. "The scale of the market loss has not been seen since the Great Depression," explained Steve Hill, who was head of the Department of Retirement Systems. "We had to make tough choices, but they were necessary to maintain the health of the plans."

Three pension-reform bills were finally passed. The changes eliminated an automatic cost-of-living adjustment for retirees in one of the oldest plans; established new, early retirement benefit-reduction factors; changed retiree return-to-work rules; and included other reforms. Hill estimates these will save $10 billion over 25 years and keep the plans financially stable and sustainable.

Washington's state employee pension plan was the nation's second strongest-funded plan in 2011, according to a report released by Morningstar, an investment research firm. That was before our last reform.

My third goal was to streamline state government's structure. As I said in my 2009 State of the State address, "Over the decades, state government has evolved—layer, upon layer, upon layer. But too much of what served people well in 1940 or 1960 or 1990 does not serve people well in the 21st century."

One of my targets was the proliferation of boards and commissions in state government. I felt certain citizens could do without groups like the Interagency Integrated Pest Management Coordinating Committee, Firearms Range Advisory Committee, Industry Cluster Advisory Committee, or Special License Plate Review Board. We were successful in eliminating nearly one-third of the 460 boards and commissions, and 22 others were restructured to save money and improve efficiency.

In 2011, to strip out layers and streamline services, I proposed consolidating five agencies that provided services to state government into one—the new Department of Enterprise Services (DES). The merger would eliminate about 100 positions, save $18 million a biennium and consolidate functions like mail service, information technology (IT), printing, personnel, motor pool and grounds crews into a central-service agency.

The campaign to create DES was truly an inside-government fight, with only the public employee unions and some legislators in fierce opposition. The union argued the bill threatened public service and hard-won bargaining rights. Some legislators said the complexity of the merger made the bill unrealistic, and they questioned whether it would improve efficiency and save money.

Despite all the talk about the need for reform in government, the bill never did have a real champion in the Democrat-controlled House.

Some called it the "sleeper bill" of the session because it remained pretty much under the radar until the final hours. On the night of May 25, with the House waiting to adjourn sine die, there was a sudden flurry of activity as the clock approached midnight. It turns out that, while there was little enthusiasm for the bill in the House, there was support in the Senate, and senators were holding the budget hostage in order to get support for the merger. To state the obvious, no budget meant legislators weren't going home.

The bill finally passed, but then a new scramble ensued. The final bill called for the consolidation to take place in just four months.

To head the reorganization and new agency, I chose Joyce Turner.

Joyce was head of the soon-to-be-abolished Department of General Administration (GA) and had the variety of experience we needed to assemble the new agency. A few years earlier, I had asked her to help start the Department of Early Learning, and she had experience in agencies that, along with GA, were targeted for merger.

To her credit, Joyce got the merger completed on time, although, given it was the largest consolidation of state functions in more than two decades, it would take many more months to iron out all the bugs.

With the opportunity for reform in the air, I also wanted to try to improve a governor's ability to tighten management across state government.

Stan Marshburn, then a deputy director at the Office of Financial Management (OFM), argued that the agency was already able to provide the governor with the ability to provide standards, policy, oversight and consistency of best practices across state government for financial matters. But no strong, centralized-policy direction existed in other important areas, including technology and human resources.

Use of state cell phones provided a sobering example of the problem. Without centralized standards and oversight, the state was paying hundreds of thousands of dollars for phones that weren't being used or were rarely used. Some agencies had inefficient calling plans and others didn't have tough standards to ensure phones were issued to employees only if it was absolutely necessary.

As a result, I successfully requested the Legislature restructure the technology and human-resource functions in state government.

We eliminated the Department of Information Systems and placed its service functions in a new agency called Consolidated Technology Services. Modeling practices in the private sector for overall IT policy direction, we created the Office of the Chief Information Officer (OCIO) and placed it in OFM. I hired a former Microsoft executive, Bharat Shyam, to develop a clear, effective IT strategy for state government.

For human resources, we eliminated the Department of Personnel (DOP). Most of its service, or back-office functions, went to DES, and the policy portion went to OFM and the Office of the State HR Director. Eva Santos, formerly the DOP director, became the HR director, where she helped set statewide policy aimed at improving hiring, pay, diversity and retention.

We finally had the ability to get more control, direction and oversight over management in state government, and we saw immediate results. Within months of creating the new OCIO, we had new cell-phone standards in place and eliminated more than 3,400 phones, put another 3,000 on cheaper plans, and rolled up about $1.7 million in savings.

Two other attempts at reform ran into a special-interest buzz-saw. Hunters, fishers and parks enthusiasts beat back my attempts to merge natural resource agencies into one agency. I believed it not only would have saved money, it also would have provided better management of our natural resources. I still do. Even though this reform failed, it has resulted in better and more coordination among these agencies on a number of issues.

I also tried to create an Office of Civil Rights by merging ethnic commissions, the Human Rights Commission, and other agencies into one cabinet-level office. I felt the idea would allow us to move away from silos where each group operated autonomously, and instead have an agency director who could help address a broad range of diversity issues more effectively.

The ethnic groups, however, believed they wouldn't be represented in a single agency and feared a loss of focus on their issues, particularly at a time when they were seeing increased threats, such as the anti-immigration laws being passed in other parts of the country. Prior to a Senate hearing on the bill, senators received a flood of phone calls from opponents. Then an overflow crowd of opponents at the hearing doomed its passage.

In the end, I would have liked to make more progress restructuring state government, but I was pleased we were able to make more reforms and close more outdated institutions than any other time in state history.

Looking back, the reform efforts will always remind me about the balance we have with government in this country. Part of the inefficiency we see is caused by the fact we have government of the people, by the people and for the people, and what some see as inefficiency, others see as a value.

One former DSHS secretary, who came to the state from Boeing, put it more succinctly: "I could run DSHS more efficiently, but it would be how I wanted to run it, not how the people wanted to run it."

Reinventing Corrections

KEEPING PEOPLE SAFE WHEN YOU
ARE LAYING OFF CORRECTIONAL WORKERS

THE LAST THING a governor needs from an agency is a surprise.

On a winter day in 2007, the Department of Corrections notified me that it would be releasing 83 criminals, including high-risk sex offenders and violent offenders, from two King County jails.

The offenders were being held in jail for violating terms of their parole. At the time, 30,000 inmates across the state were on the streets under court order to be supervised by the department's community corrections officers. When offenders violated parole they would be rounded up and placed in jail until a hearings officer could decide what to do about the violations.

Because our prisons were full, Corrections signed contracts with county jails to house the offenders until a hearings officer could decide what to do. The state contracted for 220 beds from King County, at a cost of $70 a day per bed, and had similar contracts with other counties across the state.

But as the number of state inmates rose well above the contracted level, King County clamored for relief. Finally, when the number of state inmates in the county jail rose to 304, and with no other place to house them, Corrections was forced to put the offenders back on the streets.

It was not the kind of announcement you want to make under any circumstance. It was even more difficult because I was awaiting a report on why three law enforcement officers had been killed in the previous six months by felons who had warrants for violating parole.

Our Corrections employees have a tough, dangerous job. Staff in prisons are expected to maintain peace in a facility that houses thousands of high-risk, violent offenders, many of whom are rival gang members, mentally ill or potential victims themselves. Community corrections officers go into dangerous neighborhoods, homeless shelters, overpasses and wooded areas to check on the most dangerous people in society, not knowing what awaits them.

When people watch the local news and see violent offenders sentenced in court, they assume the danger is over. The fact is that the risk of violence hasn't ended—it simply moved to the Department of Corrections.

It is a difficult job in the best of times, but it became even tougher when the recession slammed the state, and Corrections was faced with massive budget cuts.

In Washington, like most other states, Corrections had avoided budget cuts for years, and had even expanded. Suddenly, conditions changed dramatically. Over the next few years, the agency had to slash $300 million from its budget, layoff 20 percent of its staff, close three prisons, and still keep the public safe.

It was a huge challenge. Fortunately, I had two excellent Corrections secretaries—Eldon Vail and, later, Bernie Warner—who helped steer the state through the difficult times.

Their stories provide many valuable lessons about successfully managing a large agency, with a dangerous clientele, through tough times. Corrections staff credit using the budget crisis to foster innovation. But it also is a story of challenging the status quo; using data to solve problems and improve management; and using proven, evidence-based practices to change the status quo, even when that data may counter public perceptions.

Early in the recession, as I ordered the first rounds of budget cuts, Corrections made the traditional cuts, such as reducing travel, administration, support staff and equipment purchases. But as the cuts deepened, the agency found it needed to be more strategic.

In my meetings with the agency, we talked about the huge gap that existed between public expectations and what the research showed. The public expects all offenders to be supervised. And supervision of offenders had become a political hot potato as candidates vowed to be tough on criminals. That led to over-promising the public of just what could be done within the budget. Obviously, the public feels safer when all offenders are locked in prison or getting close supervision in the community. The data, though, told us a different story.

According to Corrections, research shows, as expected, that close supervision of higher-risk offenders decreased the likelihood they would commit a new crime. But the research also showed minimal supervision of lower-risk offenders would not increase risk to public safety.

The budget crisis forced us to confront the conflict between public perceptions and research findings. We realized we needed to face the reality that we couldn't supervise all offenders. More importantly, we knew we weren't getting a good return on tax dollars if we were spending them on low-risk offenders who are unlikely to reoffend.

"We had to be more strategic in how to downsize our operations, and focus resources on offenders considered at highest risk to commit a new crime," Warner explained.

To help do that, the agency convinced the Legislature to pass two laws that allowed them to end community supervision for low-risk offenders. By early 2012, the caseload had dropped from 30,000 to 15,000.

The change had a critical benefit. It dramatically reduced caseloads, allowing community corrections officers to spend more time with higher-risk offenders who were more likely to reoffend.

As the relentless recession continued to bear down, the state was facing yet another round of deep budget cuts. When you look at state budgets, the big cost-drivers are education, corrections and medical programs. Even if other parts of state government were eliminated, balancing the budget would be extremely tough. As a result, I was forced to caution that the next round of cuts could force us to eliminate all community supervision. It was a choice nobody wanted.

Secretary Warner and his executive staff decided that in order to save community corrections from being eliminated, they would have to do more than simply tweak the system. Staff called it reengineering community corrections. Their goal was to fundamentally change the way offenders are supervised.

They again turned to research. Researchers had found that it is the swiftness and certainty of sanctions—not the severity or duration—that most affects offender behavior.

A 2012 study by the Washington State Institute of Public Policy, for instance, found that incarceration had no impact on offender behavior. Offenders simply left jail after 30 or 60 days and were homeless, jobless and a greater risk to public safety.

Under the existing system, an offender on supervision who committed a violation could face a variety of sanctions. These could range from a simple reprimand to sitting in county jail for a week or two while awaiting a hearing that could result in 30, 60, 90 or 120 days in jail.

At the cost of $70 a day to be housed in the King County jail, the tab to the state quickly adds up, and, as Corrections staff notes, the old system was neither swift nor certain.

Warner explained that under the reengineered model, low-level violations, such as failure to report and testing positive for alcohol, would result in automatic sanctions of two or three days in jail. If offenders had a series of minor violations, they could face up to 30 days in jail. More serious offenses, such as possession of a firearm, were turned over to prosecutors who could file felony charges.

Studies, including a pilot project in Seattle, found offenders who faced swift and certain sanctions committed fewer violations and were less likely to commit a new crime.

Under this reengineered program, Corrections saved money since it had fewer offenders in county jails and fewer costly hearings. Total savings were about $15 million a year, even though the same number of offenders were supervised, but in a more effective way.

More change was sweeping through the Prison Division. Just like community corrections, prisons were facing a relentless surge of offenders. Prison population grew from 6,000 offenders in 1990 to more than 16,000 in 2005. Even the construction of three large, medium-security lock-ups in Aberdeen, Connell and Spokane was not enough to keep up with demand.

By 2008, there were more than 1,000 Washington offenders housed in for-profit, out-of-state prisons.

The key for us was to look for ways to make the prisons more efficient. Corrections, once again, turned to managing with good data, using evidence-based practices and finding creative, new ways to do their work.

Three prisons were closed, and inmates were moved (based on their risk) from older prisons to newer, more efficient facilities that cost less to maintain and operate.

National attention has been focused on the agency's sustainability program, which features the nation's first LEED-certified (Leadership in Energy and Environmental Design) prison at Coyote Ridge. Huge operating-cost savings have been made by: reducing solid waste sent to landfills by 43 percent; increasing recycling by 83 percent; cutting water use by 100 million gallons a year; and slashing heating and energy consumption by 29 percent.

Looking back, Corrections staff notes that never in the agency's long history—it started in territorial days—had it undergone so much change in so short a period of time.

It was an emotional time for employees. Hundreds of jobs were lost and many employees were forced to move and/or accept another job with the agency. At headquarters, whole divisions were eliminated, leaving more than 100 offices and cubicles empty.

Too often, people say government just makes the easy, across-the-board cuts. But at Corrections, staff were strategic and used innovation, good data and evidence-based practices to make tough, yet effective, choices. Despite the turmoil and personal hardships, the agency chose to do the job right. They used the crisis to make the corrections system better.

Friday Night Blues

AT THE HEIGHT of the Great Recession, Scott Jarvis, the head of the state Department of Financial Institutions (DFI), began to dread Friday nights.

Who wouldn't when you consider what he had to do. For 18 Friday nights, he was required to take on a task that resulted in people losing their jobs, hard-earned investments, reputations, and, in some cases, the only financial institution in their town.

Scott's job, you see, along with federal regulators, was to close failed banks.

Washington banks, he said, had some of the highest concentrations in construction and commercial real-estate lending in the nation.

"Unfortunately, with the precipitous decline in real-estate values, those concentrations caused massive loan charge-offs and foreclosures, and, ultimately, led to the demise of many financial institutions," he explained.

Nationally, there were 400 bank failures. In Washington, Scott and his staff had to close 17 banks and one credit union.

Those Fridays started as a typical day, Scott recalls, but, at the end of the workday, they quietly entered the banks, gathered employees and announced the bank was closing due to lack of capital. "Employees worried about losing their jobs, stockholders lost their investment in the banks, and board members and senior managers were faced with the humiliation of failure," Scott recalls.

Three small towns were left without banking services. This was especially hard on businesses that dealt with large amounts of cash each day. They now had to travel more than 40 miles for the next closest banking services.

Scott's experience was just one example of how the recession impacted agencies in new and challenging ways, and reinforced a number of lessons about managing in the public sector.

For Scott and his staff, they learned you have to be adaptable and nimble. They weren't used to bank closures where much of the challenge focused on managing the community needs and reactions. Closing banks was just the start. DFI worked to help towns reestablish banking services by working with state-chartered community banks to open branches in the towns or by offering other options like ATMs or courier services.

Staff at the Department of Revenue, meanwhile, had an entirely different recession-driven challenge, which had no clear solution.

In my early years in office, when Cindi Holmstrom headed the agency, there were clear procedures for collecting overdue tax payments. As the recession deepened, many businesses were hit hard. Not only were they struggling to find customers, but credit had dried up, making it difficult for them to survive the crisis. In some cases, businesses used their sales-tax collections to keep their doors open. Then the tax collector came calling.

"The department was caught between its tax-collection mandates and the belief we should try to help businesses through the crisis," said Brad Flaherty, a director at the agency later in my term.

In 2009, Revenue began seeing a big increase in outstanding receivables. The amount of delinquent debt jumped from $170 million to $250 million in just one year.

"Businesses that had never experienced collection issues in the past suddenly had a delinquent debt," Flaherty said.

As a result, Revenue began developing strategies to balance the need for collections with the need to help businesses survive.

The agency assumed more risk by carrying debt longer than best-practices had proven reasonable, but for many businesses it was what they needed to survive. There wasn't, however, clear guidance on making the call to extend time to pay. "It was more of an art than science," Flaherty said.

The stress from the business downturn also had an impact on Revenue staff. There were business owners who were out on the edge and getting desperate. "Our tax collectors and auditors have a difficult job. It was made even more difficult as a result of the recession. They were trying to help businesses survive while making sure there was a level playing field among competitors," Flaherty said.

Meanwhile, at the Employment Security Department (ESD), the challenge was trying to handle an overwhelming workload. ESD has always been unique. In good times, the workload is down, but it booms during the bad times.

When the economy was strong in 2007, ESD had about 219,000 unemployment insurance claimants. In the darkest days of the recession, the number jumped to 503,000. During the same time period, the number of people seeking help getting a job jumped from 260,000 to more than 366,000.

Given, as ESD managers say, the tsunami of work coming the agency's way, I am grateful that I appointed Karen Lee to head the agency in 2005. Karen and her deputy, Paul Trause (who succeeded her in 2010), were troubled by what they found and immediately began overhauling the agency.

Even before the recession began, the agency was struggling to meet the needs of its customers. There was a large backlog of unemployment claims awaiting decisions. The IT system was old, unreliable and not designed to meet the agency's business needs. There was no performance management system to measure staff performance and hold them accountable.

Because of performance issues and a lack of credibility with agency stakeholders, Karen and Paul adopted a new organizational structure, which better aligned with the vision of service to customers. Many senior-level employees were reassigned and others left the agency.

To get new ideas and new talent, managers were recruited from outside the agency. By the end of my term, nine of 10 senior leaders came from outside ESD.

A major IT network failure occurred soon after Karen and Paul arrived, resulting in the loss of critical information, including emails and files. To address the problem, they abandoned traditional agency practices and began investing in technology instead of staffing. The decision was controversial. It prevented the agency from hiring new staff and resulted in some staff reductions, but the effort paid off in a big way a few years later when the wave of unemployment hit and a record level of customers flooded the agency.

To address the performance management problems, they aggressively implemented the Government Management and Accountability Program (GMAP), which I had directed agencies to adopt. "We learned that if we were going to successfully turn this agency around, we must hold staff accountable," Trause said.

The agency established weekly GMAP meetings and set performance measures for the agency and each operating unit. They then began using data to hold people accountable, identify issues that needed to be addressed, and spotlight program-design changes to improve efficiency and effectiveness.

New managers, armed with better data, soon began to identify what Trause calls "unpleasant truths." For instance, the agency used to track and focus on job referrals, which occurred when unemployed workers came to ESD for help in getting jobs. "We were focused on increasing job referrals, not on providing services that actually helped people get stable, decent-paying jobs," he explained.

While the overhaul of ESD would take years, enough big changes were made in time to help the agency absorb the record demand for services that hit with the recession. Since the start of the Great Recession, ESD has helped nearly 877,000 individuals support themselves and their families with unemployment insurance benefits. In addition, they provided employment and training services to more than 1.1 million people, and made countless referrals to other social services.

Meanwhile, the unemployment insurance trust funds for 36 states went bankrupt and were forced to borrow from the federal government. Washington, on the other hand, maintained the healthiest fund in the nation, despite record payouts and three reductions in employer taxes over the last eight years.

Looking back, Paul is glad they had time to get management of the agency in order.

The recession delivered very different challenges to State Parks.

For many years, the state's general fund comprised the largest percentage of the agency's operating funds. But as the recession deepened and larger budget cuts were required, more and more general funds were cut from the Parks' budget.

The agency had to make dramatic cuts. About 200 of 600 jobs were eliminated. Regional offices were closed. Parks were transferred to local government. Popular programs like interpretation were all but eliminated. A dozen new park rangers, still in probationary status, were laid off.

Even full-time rangers weren't safe. In early 2012, Parks' management made the tough decision to shift more than 60 of the 189 full-time rangers to five and eight-month seasonal status. As Director Don Hoch noted, they got through the summer, but it was a situation that was not sustainable.

To keep employees informed, Don sent regular emails entitled "The Economy and Our Budget." The flow of bad news was so drawn out and relentless that there were 28 emails in the series, and staff soon began to dread opening them.

Looking at the Park's budget in terrible-budget times teed up a couple questions. First, did Parks really need to operate some of the smaller, less-iconic parks, or should they instead be transferred to local government? And second, should users pay for state parks so the general fund can instead pay for programs where there is no "buyer" of the services, such as protection of abused and neglected children or care of the mentally ill?

Both questions provided interesting lessons.

Parks took the transfer idea seriously and looked at options. In the end, five parks were transferred to local cities or county park systems. Any talk of transfer or closure beyond those five, however, was met with howls of protest. When there were suggestions that Lake Sylvia and Schafer state parks, located near Montesano and Elma, be closed or transferred, friends of the parks gathered 10,000 signatures opposing the idea.

To their credit, the opponents to the closure have formed an active friends group that helps raise money for utility costs, assists in cleanup, and holds regular events and fundraising for both parks.

As Parks staff notes, every park is in someone's backyard, and legislators, who hear the protests from constituents, fought additional transfers or closures.

Given the strong support for local parks, would the user-pay idea work?

Like most policy issues, a decision to make users pay for parks was not an easy one. Many people insisted it was time for some government functions to be self-sustaining and that those who benefit from the services should pay their way. Others reminded us that our parks represent the natural gems and heritage of our state and that at least paying for a portion of parks from the general fund is a vital, core responsibility.

In the end, I recommended, and the Legislature agreed, to wean Parks off the general fund and have users support parks by paying for a $30 annual Discover Pass or a $10 day-use fee.

By the end of my term, the Parks' financial story hadn't ended. Sale of the Discover Pass has fallen far short of needs. Don has endured a continuing struggle trying to keep parks open and rangers on the job during the budget crisis. He came to Washington from Georgia where the parks system is more entrepreneurial. Don's experience will come in handy, because the future for Parks probably will depend on the right mix of financing that includes some state funding, more entrepreneurism by Parks and user-pay programs.

While much of the public attention is on the state budget during a recession, agencies, just like families and businesses, went through their own unique challenges. To survive, we had to have directors who were flexible and creative, and who worked hard prior to the crisis to ensure their management house was in order.

Will You Marry Me?

A PERSONAL JOURNEY TO MARRIAGE EQUALITY

As GOVERNOR, I get more than 20,000 letters and emails a year. Each one is read by staff, and I take time to read a lot of them myself. Some really touch my heart.

One such letter was from a girl named Katie. "As a 16-year-old lesbian myself, who has gone to Catholic school, it has been hard for me to picture a bright future for myself," Katie wrote.

Katie was writing to thank me for my support of legislation to legalize same-sex marriage in Washington. Several weeks after my announcement, in a landmark and emotional vote, the measure passed the Legislature. "People like you are the reason I am still alive and dreaming today," Katie said, adding, "now one day I can get down on one knee and ask my girl not 'Will you civil union me?' but 'Will you marry me?'"

I was surprised by the number of emails and letters I received—the vast majority in support. I found out later that clips of my announcement to introduce the bill and an interview with CNN had been posted on social media sites around the world, and that prompted responses from across the United States, Canada, Sweden, Australia and United Kingdom.

My position on gay marriage evolved over the years. It was a personal journey for me. Now, in retrospect, as I look back at that journey, I also realize how important that kind of evolution in thinking is for a governor, or anyone for that matter. The concept of a journey means we are open to new ideas, that we are listening, really listening, to others, and are open to new ways to see the world.

When I first ran for governor in 2004, I said, and believed, that Washington state was not ready to support gay marriage.

The state, meanwhile, was on its own journey.

In 2006, I signed legislation banning discrimination based on sexual orientation in employment, housing and other areas. Then, in 2007, I supported and signed legislation creating the state domestic partnership registry. Another step was made in 2008, when I signed legislation granting additional rights and responsibilities relating to issues such as dissolutions, community property, estate planning, taxes, court process, conflicts of interest for public officials and guardianships. Opponents unsuccessfully tried to have the law thrown out at the ballot box, but voters made Washington the first state in the nation to approve domestic partnerships.

Then 2009 brought the "anything but marriage law," which requires state agencies to ensure that all privileges, immunities, rights, benefits or responsibilities granted to married individuals are granted to an individual who is or was in a state-registered domestic partnership.

Through those years, I was never really comfortable with my position on same-sex marriage. The issue always has been a battle for me because my religion, legal training and conviction for equality were in conflict. I am a Catholic and always felt it was the church's right to make the call about marriage.

Late in 2011, I confronted the marriage issue and I found my thinking evolving. This internal debate was deeply personal. I didn't talk with staff about it. I didn't ask for briefing papers. I didn't call people in to discuss it. I did, however, listen to my daughters and recalled reports of bullying gay students. I saw gay friends and families and the love they shared.

But as I began to reach a conclusion, I did do one thing. On Thanksgiving weekend, I asked my daughters to join me for a private talk. When I told them I was going to support a gay marriage bill, they both burst out crying.

Like most of their generation, my daughters strongly support gay marriage. Unlike my generation, they grew up knowing kids on the playground who had two moms or two dads. Some of their best friends are gay. As we talked, I realized my daughters see sexual-orientation discrimination just as unacceptable as my generation viewed racial discrimination.

As my thinking evolved, I concluded the state's role was just to issue marriage licenses, and that the state should not discriminate based on sexual orientation. If we deny same-sex couples the right to marry, and say that domestic partnership is the same as marriage, we are traveling the same course as those who backed the discriminatory separate-but-equal argument that was used to keep African Americans in separate schools, lines and places.

While the state should not discriminate, I also concluded it is up to churches to make their own call about gay marriages.

Our country has slowly, over many years, broken down discriminatory barriers against racial minorities, women, people with disabilities and others. Now is the time, I concluded, for us to take the next step in expanding equality.

Some people have suggested I took my stand in support of same-sex marriages only because I decided not to run again and wouldn't have to deal with the political fallout. Nothing could be further from the truth. While some people believe politicians take only the politically safe positions, we can—and should—take personal, intellectual journeys that can change our stance on issues.

On a personal level, my decision on the marriage bill had a significant effect. For the first time in eight years, I felt good about my position.

So on Feb. 13, 2012, I was honored to sign the marriage legislation before an overflow crowd of marriage advocates and media in the ornate state reception room.

"As governor for more than seven years, this is one of my proudest moments," I told the crowd.

Looking out at an audience with many tear-filled eyes, I added, "And most surely today is a proud day in the history of the Legislature and the state of Washington. It is a day historians will mark as a milestone for equal rights. A day when we did what was right, we did what was just, and we did what was fair. We stood up for equality and we did it together—Republicans and Democrats, gay and straight, young and old, and a variety of religious faiths. I'm proud of who and what we are in this state."

It was a tense journey to get to that historic day. There were many courageous votes by legislators who supported the bill despite opposition from vocal constituents back home. Special credit goes to Sen. Ed Murray and Rep. Jamie Pedersen who steered the bill through the Senate and House, respectively.

Once again, opponents tried to have the law overturned by voters, but, on Election Day 2012, Washington, Maryland and Maine became the first states in the nation to approve same-sex marriages at the polls.

Six months after passage of the marriage bill, I was asked to be grand marshal of the Gay Pride Parade in Seattle. As we rolled down the street, I noticed one elderly gentleman sitting in a chair curbside. His conservative clothing stood out among all the boas, sequins, leather and spiked heels worn by many parade marchers.

As my car neared, I watched two young men help the elderly man to his feet, and, as my car passed, he straightened to attention and gave me a crisp salute.

It may have taken me a while to complete my journey on gay marriage, but for that gentleman, for Katie and for all the couples who want to say they are married to the person they love, I am thankful to have completed it in time to help fight discrimination and advance equality.

Under Siege

FOR ME, the unsung players in state government during the Great Recession were its employees.

One of the most discouraging aspects of state government's troubled journey through the recession was the fervor with which some newspaper editorial pages, commentators and politicians demanded even deeper cuts to employee pay and benefits, as if that were the solution to the economic crisis.

I can understand the frustration many people felt during the difficult days of the recession. People were losing their jobs, businesses and homes. Suddenly, moms and dads were struggling to find ways to feed their families, pay the utility bills, cover medical expenses, or buy a winter jacket for their child.

Many former state employees were in that same predicament. More than 7,500 state workers were laid off during the recession. Many of those who were able to keep their jobs were helping those families in trouble by providing unemployment insurance payments, arranging for food stamps, or getting families help paying utility bills.

Not only did thousands of state workers lose their jobs, many more were forced to move to keep their jobs. Others were "bumped" into lower positions. Programs they cared passionately about were gutted. Every year for four years, they worried about whether this time or this budget would spell the end of their job or their spouse's job.

Almost all families had to make sacrifices during the recession. State employees were no exception. They went more than four years without an increase in pay. As the crisis deepened, they agreed to a two-year, 3 percent pay cut. There was a five-fold increase in their share of insurance premiums; out-of-pocket health-care costs increased by more than $300 a year; and they contributed more to their pension plan.

One budget-cutting idea involved requiring unpaid furloughs for state workers. Implementing the idea, however, quickly created problems. Managers soon realized it was a problem taking many state workers, like prison guards, off the job. As a result, so many exemptions had to be granted that only about a third of all general government employees were required to take furlough days, and we ended up with gross inequality in applying dramatic pay cuts across the workforce.

Despite all the anguish and turmoil, employees *agreed* to pay cuts. They never went on strike. They labored on through changing, disruptive working conditions and a rapidly swelling workload.

The workforce shrunk, but not the workload. Today, compared to 2001, there are 2,000 fewer state employees to serve one million more Washington residents.

Unfortunately, in some states, bashing public employees has become politically fashionable, which seems strange to me since almost everyone's life is touched by them.

Why would we bash people who put themselves in great danger to keep us safe? Two of the saddest memories from my time as governor are of memorial services for two state employees. Washington State Patrol Trooper Tony Radulescu, who also served in the Army, was killed in 2012 during a traffic stop in Gorst, Kitsap County.

Like most public employees, Tony believed his work made a difference. "Many people wonder an entire lifetime whether or not they made a difference," Washington State Patrol Chief John Batiste said at the service. "As a soldier and trooper, Tony never had to worry about that."

The other service was for Jayme Biendl, a 34-year-old correctional officer who was strangled to death by an inmate at Monroe Correctional Complex.

When people are convicted of crimes and sent to prison, they may be out of our communities, but it is only because public employees like Jayme are willing to serve.

At Jayme's service, Corrections Secretary Eldon Vail reminded us that officers like Jayme work a hard, dangerous job that is under-appreciated and often misunderstood. "No one knows how hard the work is except those who do it," he said.

Why would we bash child welfare workers who spend their days in the darkest corners of our world helping vulnerable children escape a life of abuse and neglect? As a young attorney for the Attorney General's Office, I worked with case workers and saw their files filled with horrific cases of children broken and bruised physically and mentally. Yet those case workers came to work every day intent on making life better for a child in need.

Why would we bash workers who are protecting our health? Department of Health employees at the Public Health Laboratories conduct important tests daily for diseases like tuberculosis and flu. They take the initiative to go beyond the testing. Lab Director Dr. Romesh Gautom led the development of a faster test for E. coli bacteria. His work reduced the test times from several days to one, which is precious time saved in the world of disease investigation. His new technique is now used around the world.

Why would we bash our transportation maintenance crews who work in the snow, wind, rain and dark of night alongside traffic to keep our roads open and safe? Some of those workers, like Harry Nelson and Terry Kukes, will literally go the extra mile for people.

In 2011, the two were informed that a family lost a teddy bear during an unexpected stop along Interstate 90. The bear had been given to a young girl by her father who had been deployed overseas. The two searched for the lost bear, found it, and then drove from Ellensburg to Sedro-Woolley—350 miles round trip—on their own time and their own dime to deliver the bear.

Why would we bash people like Becky Larson, the receptionist in my office who calmly, patiently and gracefully takes thousands of calls every year and keeps government accessible—even to the crankiest, angriest and most difficult people?

Fortunately, there are those who do recognize the contributions of public employees. On March 4, 2012, The *Herald* in Everett ran an editorial headlined "More thanks, less blame."

"Public employees, particularly those who work in state government, can be excused for feeling a bit under siege lately," the editorial noted.

"These days, they shoulder too much blame for budgets that are out of whack. Whether it's over collective bargaining rights, pension benefits or health insurance plans, state employees are unfairly singled out as a problem," it noted.

The paper said, "The overwhelming majority of them deserve the gratitude of the public they serve," and it went on to note the tragic deaths of Tony, Jayme and three other public employees.

Like The *Herald* said, state salaries, pensions and benefits are all fair game for open, honest debate. But the debate should focus on the facts. It's not okay to slip into the trap of thinking we can demand vital services but then not pay people an honest day's wage for an honest, tough day of work.

For me, President Kennedy issued a call to serve and I gladly answered that call. I have proudly served for more than 40 years with fellow state employees. Public service is a career that doesn't make you rich financially, but it leaves you rich with memories of giving back and making life better for others.

My greatest fear is that the attacks on public employees will result in good people turning away from state service. We need a new generation to answer JFK's call and begin the hard work of helping make Washington a great state to live.

ACKNOWLEDGEMENTS

I REMEMBER taking a few days off after my re-election in November 2008. The only work-related reading I brought was a copy of Governor Clarence Martin's inaugural address made in 1933 as the economic fallout of the Great Depression was reaching its height in Washington.

At the time of my vacation, our state, like the rest of the nation, was sinking into a recession that would later turn out to be the greatest economic downturn since the Great Depression. I brought Governor Martin's speech to try to get ideas about how a former governor had managed in a recession. His remarks were the only document I could find that offered clues—in this case, however, limited—about managing state government in difficult financial times.

That's when my thoughts about this book began. As the recession deepened and our problems grew more difficult by the month, I was more convinced that I wanted to leave some record that might be useful to future governors or students of government.

Producing the book made me reflect about more than lessons learned. I realized more than ever that any success a governor has is a measure of the kind of people he or she has around them. I was fortunate to have outstanding cabinet directors and staff who helped me work through the issues outlined in this book, and then helped me retell the stories.

My husband, Mike, daughter, Courtney, and her husband Scott Lindsay, and daughter, Michelle, have provided me the love and support that helped carry me through the eight years as governor. They served as sounding boards and advisers. They encouraged me, challenged me, and raised my spirits in the tough times. They kept me rooted and humble. I know they had to make a lot of sacrifices, but they never complained and they were always there for me. Every governor should have a family like them.

Special thanks to Fred Olson who has worked with me for 24 years. We have been through a lot together and it was only appropriate that he help me capture some of the lessons learned during our last eight years. He is a talented writer who worked tirelessly on this effort. It could not have happened without him.

I deeply appreciate the work Kari Burrell, my policy director, did to organize ideas, materials and interviews for the book and the editing work done by Kym Ryan, Kate Lykins-Brown and Dustin Terpening.

I am indebted to those who served on my senior staff. They have been an extremely dedicated group with tough jobs, because any issue that is worked in a governor's office is complex and highly contentious with sharply different viewpoints between interest groups. While most attention is focused on the senior staff, I would be remiss not to thank the rest of my staff, including receptionists and the wonderful employees in our Constituent Services Unit who handle thousands of calls, letters, emails and walk-ins every year. They are the face of a governor's office and are the ones who provide the lasting impression of our office for most people.

My executive assistant, Ellen Landino, and scheduler, Barb Winkler, were extraordinary in their dedication and day-to-day assistance to me.

A special thanks also to my cabinet, with a particular nod to those who, in early 2005, were willing to give up other jobs and join my administration even though my narrow election victory was being challenged in court. You will see examples of the kinds of challenges and issues cabinet directors faced in this book. These stories, however, touch on just a fraction of their work, which was always carried out with great professionalism, balance of all competing viewpoints and high ethical standards.

Like any business executive, a governor needs great managers around them—selecting a cabinet must be done with great care.

I was blessed with a great policy team. A governor will face a staggering range of issues in any given year and he or she needs policy advisers who can quickly summarize the issue, and the various viewpoints and options available.

In the budget section of the book, you will see my great appreciation for my budget staff at the Office of Financial Management. I think it is safe to say no budget staff in Washington state history has gone through a more grueling, emotional, four-year period than the wonderful crew I worked with.

There also is a chapter on state employees, and I think my thanks and admiration for these wonderful people bears repeating. They have tough jobs in normal circumstances, but, like their counterparts in the private sector, the recession made their work even tougher (if they were able to keep their jobs). I am proud to have served alongside them.

There is another group that I also need to acknowledge. They aren't on my team, but they are obviously key players in the drama of state government—the Legislature. By the very nature of our form of government, there will be tension between the executive and Legislature. There are going to be battles over politics and the best public policy direction for Washington. In almost all cases, though, I found legislators willing to put previous disagreements behind us and move on to the next fight. Ultimately, we worked together and that was vital to the state, especially in the difficult recession years.

I leave office with a profound respect for the Legislature and the people who served there. Most of the accomplishments cited in this book were done in partnership with members of the House and Senate.

A special thanks also to Dean Sandra Archibald at the University of Washington's Evans School for Public Affairs. Sandra encouraged me to write this book and arranged for students, under the leadership of Professor Joaquin Herranz, to help with research. Those students were Audrey Peek, Ben Landsman, Christopher Jordan, Haley Harguth, Kiana Scott, Lindsay J. Fromme, Michael Moran, Terry Sullivan and Varsha Khanna.

The Washington State Heritage Center Trust works to keep our state's rich and varied history alive and accessible. The support, advice and help the staff gave to me for this project is deeply appreciated.

And finally, a special thanks to Weyerhaeuser Company, PEMCO Insurance and Microsoft for their donations to the Trust that made printing this book possible.